Champagne Luncheon

with

Judith Leiber

Best Wishes
Judith Leiber

Compliments of
U.S. TRUST

JUDITH LEIBER

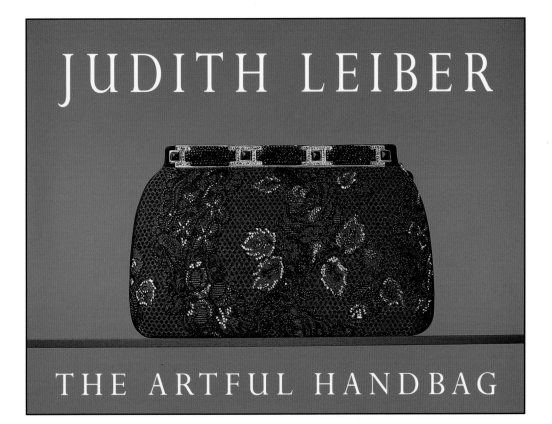

THE ARTFUL HANDBAG

JUDITH LEIBER

THE ARTFUL HANDBAG

TEXT BY

ENID NEMY

PRINCIPAL PHOTOGRAPHY BY

JOHN BIGELOW TAYLOR

HARRY N. ABRAMS, INC., PUBLISHERS

Judith Leiber gratefully acknowledges Swarovski Crystal for its
generous contribution to the preparation of this book.

This book is dedicated to my beloved husband, Gus, whose help and
enthusiastic support made this all possible.
—Judith Leiber

*Page 1: Black and gold French brocade, aurum and rhinestone re-embroidery, 1993; Page 3: Pearl nautilus shell with gold-plated
lid (Collection The Metropolitan Museum of Art, New York), 1972; Page 6: Gray patent leather box bag with double closure, 1985;
Page 7: (top) Two lovebird locks on green suede, rounded frame clutch, drop-in chain, 1992; (bottom) Teardrop-shaped box
with winding snake design, python pattern, drop-in chain, 1981*

Editor: Beverly Fazio Herter
Designers: Carol A. Robson with Gilda Hannah

Library of Congress Cataloging-in-Publication Data
Nemy, Enid.
  Judith Leiber, the artful handbag / text by Enid Nemy ; photographs by
John Bigelow Taylor.
    p. cm.
    ISBN 0–8109–3571–6. —ISBN 0–8109–2609–1 (pbk.)
    1. Handbags—Exhibitions. 2. Handbags—Pictorial works—
Exhibitions. 3. Leiber, Judith—Exhibitions. I. Taylor, John Bigelow.
II. Leiber, Judith. III. Title.
TT667.N45 1994   94–17787
746.9'2—dc20

Published in 1995 by Harry N. Abrams, Incorporated, New York

Printed and bound in China
10 9 8 7 6 5

Harry N. Abrams, Inc.
100 Fifth Avenue
New York, NY 10011
www.abramsbooks.com

Abrams is a subsidiary of
LA MARTINIÈRE
G R O U P E

Sleeping cat, chalk, hematite, and clear rhinestones,
1984

CONTENTS

Foreword

Judith Leiber loves designing handbags. This became clear after my first visit to her showroom. Hundreds and hundreds of handbags, each beautifully and impeccably made, spill out of armoires, fill every windowsill, cluster in every corner of the room. Her passion is equally apparent on a tour of the adjoining workshops, where all of the bags are made under her watchful eye. As she stops and confers, in several languages, with her crafts people, she demonstrates her thorough knowledge of making handbags.

Judith Leiber is known best for her bejeweled evening bags and minaudières . . . a whimsical menagerie of dogs and cats; turtles, fish, and real shells, as well as tiny suitcases, books, and folding fans; fruit, vegetables, and eggs. Collectors find these treasures irresistible. They are witty little sculptures, appealing objects of adornment.

The Museum at the Fashion Institute of Technology is honored to present the exhibition *Judith Leiber: The Artful Handbag*. This talented designer, who is celebrating thirty years of work, embodies all that the school teaches. Her creativity is manifest not only in the art and design of her handbags but also in their technical excellence and her skillful marketing. She has established a successful business, producing her handbags here in New York. A most highly respected designer of accessories, Judith Leiber has made a major contribution to the prominence of American fashion.

Judith Leiber never tires of designing handbags. Each new idea is a delight and each new bag triggers further variations, new directions. "Here is the leopard pattern on an egg. Have I shown you our new Humpty Dumpty?" She tells me proudly, "Now we are doing the tomato in orange and it will be a pumpkin! We are a crazy bunch!"

Multicolored grouse box, drop-in chain, 1985

DOROTHY TWINING GLOBUS
DIRECTOR
THE MUSEUM AT THE FASHION INSTITUTE
OF TECHNOLOGY

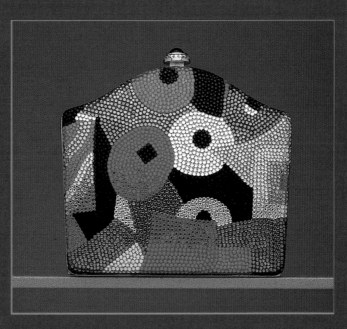

Pop art-inspired box, onyx lock, drop-in chain,
1990

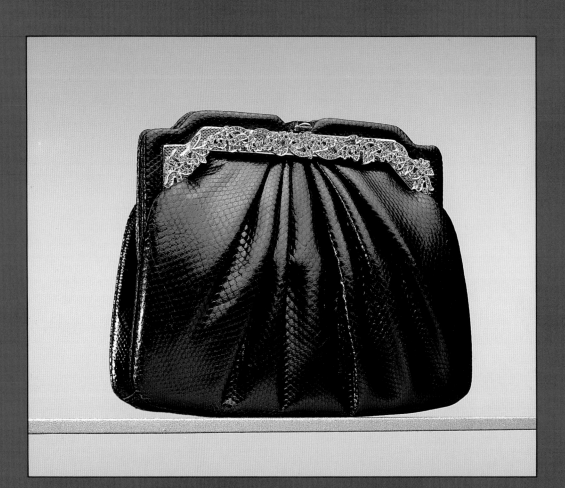

*Rhinestone decorated frame on gathered clutch
made of black karung snake, 1978*

*Lucite bar with rhinestone decorations on black
suede classic frame clutch, 1994*

*Left: blue satin tote with rhinestone ring handles, 1975;
right: black suede frame bag with tubular rhinestone handle, 1993*

*Black and clear rhinestone geometric patchwork
on rounded box, onyx lock, 1990*

"Smoke" Lucite box with gold-plated frame and shoulder chain
(Collection The Metropolitan Museum of Art, New York), 1972

*Ebony box inspired by Japanese inro
with cinnabar balls and passementerie handle
(Collection The Metropolitan Museum of Art, New York), 1979*

*Ebony box carved in India with vermeil closing, 1977.
From the collection of Beverly Sills*

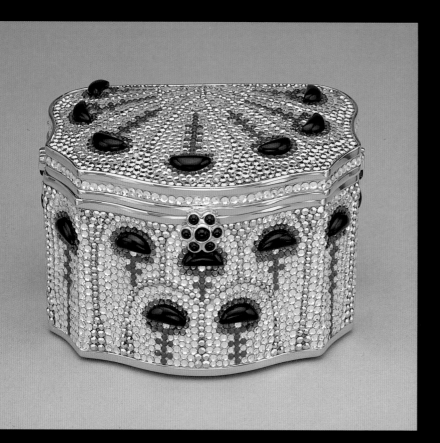

*Tiny "sweetmeat box" peacock pattern with large onyx
cabochons, drop-in chain, 1979*

I

The Art of the Handbag

Judith Leiber with Stanley Marcus, the presenter of the Lifetime Achievement Award from the Council of Fashion Designers of America, at Lincoln Center, February 7, 1994

Her designs inspire the same sense of wonder, delight, and awe as a Fabergé egg or a Schlumberger jewel. Calling Judith Leiber an accessory designer is what one museum curator described as "a little like calling Louis Comfort Tiffany a designer of lighting fixtures."

She's not an artist, she says, but her creations are closer to art than fashion, a cult among the cognoscenti, each as easily identifiable and as distinctive in its own way as a Renoir or Picasso.

The Leiber bags reflect the intellect of their creator. The designs for day are masterpieces of sophistication, fashioned in luxurious suedes, buttery leathers, polished and buffed reptile skins. The evening confections are jewels, witty, whimsical, and unashamedly extravagant, embedded with thousands of individually hand-set rhinestones. Most of them bring forth an automatic smile. "You have to kid people a little, make them laugh," she says.

They are meant to be coddled in a hand, slung over a shoulder, or, in a few cases, worn around the neck. Many glitter in the permanent collections of museums, and many more are in the private collections of women who treat them as *objets* and display them in vitrines, étageres, and specially built cases.

She's mentioned in a current novel about New York as someone whose name lends cachet. "He knew Judith Leiber, the handbag designer, personally," one of the characters says.

Her bags are automatic subjects of conversation and instant icebreakers at cocktail and dinner parties. "When I'm wearing one of her egg designs, people ask me if it's a Fabergé egg," Beverly Sills said. "To me it's just as valuable, it's a Leiber egg."

Geoffrey Beene, who has specially designed Leiber handbags in his Fifth Avenue boutique (the only non-Beene the boutique carries) calls them "objects of desire." Of Mrs. Leiber, he says simply, "Her work is unique."

At big charity events, women who leave their Leiber evening bags on the table when they get up to dance return to find other guests standing there, admiring the designs. Occasionally, bags temporarily disappear. Friends borrow them to show at other tables and often they're then passed around the room.

Many of the Leiber creations look as though they're spun of dreams and some are, but despite three decades in a capricious business, the spinner is down-to-earth. She enjoys hearing about the various ways her bags are used but she isn't carried away.

"I'd rather have a Henry Moore maquette on my table than a Judith Leiber cat," she says. In fact, there are several Henry Moores and no Leibers on the tables in her two homes.

Still, practicality doesn't diminish pride. She never attends a social event without making a mental note of the number of Leiber bags swinging from shoulders or clutched in hands. Occasionally, especially on opening night but also on other occasions, she and her husband stand in the lobby of the Metropolitan Opera House and count the number of her designs being carried. Mr. Leiber, with understandable pride and perhaps just a little exaggeration, suggests that it has now reached the point where it might be easier to count the non-Leiber bags.

"Seeing my bags at the opera is, to me, in a very minor way, like being one of the performers," she once said. "It's my share of applause. Those women carrying my bags seem to be saying, 'Bravo, Judy.'"

If there aren't enough Leiber handbags at any event she attends, she doesn't take it lightly. Why aren't there? What percentage would be enough? she's asked. "One hundred," she says in her still Hungarian-accented English ("I used to speak British English with a Hungarian accent," she says. "My husband changed me to American English with a Hungarian accent.") Then she grins to show that she doesn't mean it—but maybe she does. Realistically? How can she answer such a question—however many there are, there should be more.

The women who own, and very often collect, Leiber bags are, for the most part, affluent. Some are active in the volunteer world and others have top-level careers in business and the arts. These women wear designer dresses and real jewelry, or costume jewelry so good and so expensive that it looks real. But a surprising number of Leiber owners are in less exalted financial brackets. They are mid-level career women who sacrifice other purchases to buy one bag, some because they can't resist a particular design, some because the bag adds an aura to the rest of their outfit, and some simply for status, although there are no blatant identifying initials.

Her handbags are her children, Mrs. Leiber says, "and they don't talk back." She loves them, admittedly some more than others. She's proud of them, although a few don't turn out the way she expects. And just like many a proud—and strict—parent, she doesn't allow them to leave her roost looking less than their best.

She has found inspiration in books and animals, Oriental carpets and quilts, paintings and Foo dogs, James Bond movies and stained glass, tapestries and tomatoes. And even her personal preferences and expeditions—museums, music, yard sales, antiquing, traveling—serve a dual purpose. As with many artists, ideas spring to mind everywhere, suddenly and unexpectedly. One day, she was shown a friend's teddy bear collection, and after announcing or, as she is sometimes apt to do, pronouncing, that a grown woman collecting teddy bears was "ridiculous," she took another look. Well, maybe she was a bit hasty, she said—could she borrow one? And that's how the teddy bear bag was born.

Occasionally she's inspired by the cut of clothes, but more often it's a museum or antique sale that sparks an idea. An Oriental incense burner developed into her resting crane handbag and an antique ivory baby pacifier bought at a Madison Square Garden show resulted in the rabbit bag. The Matisse show led to a number of floral designs, a Japanese cat in front of a fireplace became a gold metal feline, and a Buddha sculpture is now an inscrutable but sparkly metal face.

What can evolve from a Russian stamp box? A lion sitting atop an evening bag. The Duchess of Windsor's jewels? A number of interesting animals. A nineteenth-century cookie tin? A glittering multihued scaled-down box.

Mrs. Leiber loves cooking and food, the latter perhaps more than the former, so her handbags modeled on fruits and vegetables didn't require anything more than her table for inspiration. There are, to date, watermelon, grapefruit, and lemon slices, tomato, pumpkin, and eggplant designs—broccoli isn't being considered, but who knows?

Possibly the most unusual group of bags in the showroom is that based on the cities of America. There's Chicago's Old Water Tower framed by a skyline studded with crystal stars, New York's Empire State Building and skyline, the famous Hollywood Hill sign for the village that was once the hub of the movie business, and Boston's Cape Cod cousin. Recently European cities joined the group—Paris and its Eiffel Tower and the top of the Spanish steps in Rome were added, with London yet to come.

One of Mrs. Leiber's prettiest bags—a lotus bud—came from an actual lotus bud in the garden of Jack Lenor Larsen, the fabric designer, and one of her latest innovations was inspired by Mr. Beene. He designed a dress she wore to the 1994 awards ceremony of the Council of Fashion Designers of America, at which she was the first handbag designer to be honored with an award.

"Why don't you wear your handbag as a piece of jewelry?" he suggested, and this led to the "jewel in hand" becoming a "jewel-around-the-neck." Mrs. Leiber designed a small ovoid-shaped gray hematite bag, embellished it with a spanking white daisy and wore it, to considerable astonishment and admiration, as a large pendant necklace.

Leiber designs are expensive; superb craftsmanship and meticulous detailing do not come cheap. "Her incomparable handbags truly merit the appellation of

White pearl beaded teddy bear, 1992

*Gold-plated pig with onyx eyes and nostrils
and drop-in chain, 1991*

museum quality," says JoAnne Olian, consultant curator to the costume collection of the Museum of the City of New York.

"Sensuous and tactile, they ask to be picked up," is how they are described by Dorothy Twining Globus, director of the Museum at the Fashion Institute of Technology. "I am amazed to find myself wanting to try out each bag . . . to feel its weight, see how the clasp works, explore the inside."

Mrs. Leiber is a designer in love with what she does. She loves the smell of leather, the feel of fabrics, the light points shooting out from boxes of rhinestones, the colored threads that twist and loop into embroidery and patchwork. She is, in fact, among the fortunate—those who look forward to going to work in the morning and leave somewhat regretfully at the end of the day.

As businesses go, the Leiber firm is small but growing, with annual sales of about twenty-five thousand handbags. Measured on another basis, however—a retail price range of $700 to $7,000—this small business is nonetheless lucrative.

Mrs. Leiber creates five collections a year, in all about one hundred designs, some completely new and others distinct variations on classics and popular patterns.

Any failures? Of course, although she prefers a more down-to-earth word. "About twenty or so are bummers," she says. Successful designs go in and out of collections, sometimes merely as a matter of change for the sake of change; other times designs that coordinate particularly well with current fashion are revived. One of the designs still selling well is a fairly simple rhinestone-handled evening bag that has been successful since the early years of the business. A design based on a Victorian soap dish has had a slightly bumpier career—it was in, then out, and now it's back again.

At times, when Mrs. Leiber finds a frame or ornament of particular appeal, she will reverse her usual procedure and shape the bag around it, showing off the frame to its best advantage.

Judith Leiber, Inc., is situated in a modest building in an unprepossessing street off Manhattan's Fifth Avenue, just around the corner from the Empire State Building. It is the traditional handbag area, surrounded by drab structures, loading docks, fast-food restaurants, street vendors, and oddment stores—gray and cold in the winter, blistering with heat in the summer.

The fourth floor Leiber offices and showroom are an oasis in these mundane surroundings. Concealed lighting highlights the rosy beige ambiance, the lithographs of Mr. Leiber's art, the curved wooden chairs, ornate, hand-painted bamboo pieces, inlaid tables, and palm trees. But with all the incidentals and interesting, decorative furniture, there is no question where the eyes alight, mesmerized. That's assuming they are able to alight. There's a problem here, some four hundred handbags in armoires and glass cases, or strategically placed at corners of the thickly carpeted floor, or on Lucite pedestals and tables and, together with a collection of uniquely buckled belts, hanging from screens.

Where to look first—the oversized polished alligator tote on the floor, the jeweled confection that's shaped like a trio of books, the plump tomato sparkling as it never did in field or kitchen, the glittering cuddly panda, the egg-head Humpty-Dumpty, with naked feet, pantaloons, and a bow on his belly? Just a moment! Is that a butterfly resting on its rhinestones, making friends with a witty little ladybug? And could Grandma ever visualize what's happened to her taken-for-granted old quilt? Probably not. It's hard even today to associate the quilted, beaded, altogether glamorous handbag with the homey bed covering of yesteryear.

It is almost impossible—although most often necessary—to choose just one Leiber handbag. Mrs. Leiber herself owns about twenty-five—at a time. However, unlike most of her customers, she gets bored with the same designs. "Something new comes up," she says. In fact, one of her major regrets is that the women who own Leiber bags don't get bored with them and that the bags rarely wear out. "They last too long," she says with a combination of pride and regret.

Her own favorite style is a comparatively small rounded clutch that, with no logic, she says, "makes me feel like a little girl—and skinnier."

"I love bags that are soft in feel yet stand up," she says. "My ideal is a bag that a woman stuffs all her things in and that still looks the way it did when she took it out of the box. It should look sleek even when stuffed."

Still, she admits that there is a limit to stuffing. And she's well aware that if there is any criticism of her evening bags, it's that many of the metal designs are so small they hold very little. She's aware but unconcerned. It hasn't detracted from their popularity and, even more important, she says that all one needs to carry in the evening is a lipstick, handkerchief, and a $100 bill. As for a comb (although she does supply a tiny one in each of her bags), eyeglasses, keys—what's an escort for? And that $100 bill, which isn't small change—chances are if you can afford a Leiber bag, a $100 bill is also manageable. Mind you, if it's changed into smaller denominations at some point in the evening, the thickness of the wad would be a hurdle in some of the designs.

For day, her view is that "if it's necessary to carry alot, the ideal is a big bag with a small one inside." It's advice she heeds herself. The bag she uses most is her alligator tote, but she usually doesn't need a small bag inside because, if the need arises, she can always borrow one from one of the shelves.

Clockwise from left:
jet and rhinestone "Hollywood" minaudière with onyx lock, 1978; star-shaped rhinestone box, 1994;
New York skyline, 1978; star pillbox, 1994

Three book bags encrusted with rhinestones. Top: black and rhinestone tartan pattern;
left: "Chinese sleeve" embroidery pattern;
right: geometric design in black, red, and clear rhinestones. All 1991

The alligator used in Leiber bags is American but is sent off to Italy for tanning, a procedure that is obviously an expensive one. This necessity for Italian tanning came about when American alligator was put on the endangered species list in the 1970s; as a result many tanneries went out of business. When, in the 1980s, alligators became so prolific they were literally crawling out of the bayous into houses, most of the tanneries remained closed and the relevant skills had been lost.

"Alligators are fair game again," Mrs. Leiber said, "but we still have to send the skins to Europe."

Almost all the Leiber bags, even those with handles, have shoulder straps tucked away, some detachable and others permanently affixed but, when need be, unseen. Also, wrapped in tissue and tucked way in each bag, are a small round mirror, edged in gold or silver metal, and a tiny matching comb, the Leiber name discreetly etched on both. The tasseled comb is more fun than practical—an elegant conversation piece that would have a hard time smoothing more than a few strands of hair.

The comb and mirror, the flannel pouch, the bed of tissue, and the gray patterned-reptile box that denotes a Leiber design are the final touches in an operation that employs more than two hundred people and requires anywhere from one to two years from the conception of an idea to a finished bag. One of the reasons for the time span is that most of the bags have from seventy-five to one hundred parts, some of which are manufactured in Europe. Another is that almost every operation is done by hand.

The Leiber day bags encompass many styles. The bucket is her version of the carpet bag, the body bag is an interpretation of the backpack. There's a bag that looks like a lunch box—a lunch box such as there never was, needless to say—and one, long and rounded, that is called an umbrella case. There are small and large envelopes, zippered bags with side pockets, and even a 007 James Bond bag that has a secret compartment at the bottom.

Some one hundred women are engaged in doing nothing but beading the minaudières, the bags for which Mrs. Leiber is particularly noted. There is a babble of languages in the workrooms, with an emphasis on Spanish, as each minuscule rhinestone is picked up with jeweler's tweezers, touched to an adhesive, and individually glued onto a design that has already been outlined on the bag in color. Each bag requires between seven thousand and thirteen thousand rhinestones, imported from the Tyrol section of Austria and made by Swarovski, the company that cut the chandeliers of New York's Metropolitan Opera House. The beading operation alone, generally divided among two or more workers, takes the equivalent of two to five days of work.

For leather and fabric bags, the first operation consists of cutting a paper pattern and then cutting every part of the bag, completely by hand, in whatever material is being used. After that, the skins or fabric are gathered, folded, shirred, quilted, or trapunto puffed before marriage to their interlinings and later attachment to their frames. Whenever a pattern requires bending or stitching, the leather is skived, or thinned, to the necessary degree. If a fabric is used, particularly a tartan, each section is carefully matched.

A latex machine, similar to one utilized in shoe factories, is used only for putting interlinings together. The interlinings are one of the truly hidden secrets of a Leiber bag, with as many as seven in a single design. Among the interlinings used are paper, muslin, flannel, horsehair, foam rubber, canvas, and wadding. All of them go into some bags and at least several go into every bag. The soft bags usually take an extra layer of a stiff material.

Once the interlinings are put together, they are cemented to the outside material by hand and the various parts are sewn together. Many operations—shirring is one—that theoretically could be done by machine, are done by hand so that the leather remains soft. Machine work for such details can work well but the outcome is more chancy, a risk Mrs. Leiber is not prepared to take. If the bag is a soft one, it is piped, turned over, and the lining—silk or leather—is dropped in, not quite literally but almost. Backed by the multi-interlinings, the lining is, to a great degree, what makes the difference between a sleek bag and one without distinctive form.

Mrs. Leiber, who is not slow to say what she thinks, controls herself when exclamations of surprise, and sometimes disbelief, are voiced about the number of parts and, equally, the number of interlinings, in each bag. "People think you take two pieces of leather and put them together," she says. There's usually an accompanying shrug that indicates that she's heard it all before and if you don't believe her, *tant pis.*

The frames, some imported from Italy and Spain, some inspired by frames seen at antique shows and auctions, are, in some cases, decorative in themselves and, in other instances, enhanced with semiprecious stones. There are hundreds and, over the years there have been thousands of different shapes and styles, but in some intangible way there is something about each of them that immediately identifies it as a Leiber bag. The stones used in the frames and also in the clasps are semiprecious, not colored glass. Among them are—name any one and it's probably on the list—tiger's eye, lapis, onyx, amethyst, jade, rose quartz, hematite, sodalite, garnet, malachite, agate, faux pearl, and carnelian. At one time, small, real (precious as opposed to semiprecious) stones were used in some bags but the practice was quickly discontinued when it was discovered that it was

A group of seashell-shaped boxes. Left: 1979; center: 1986; right: 1993; pillbox: 1992

Fan-shaped minaudières, top inspired by a swan, left and right geometric patterns. All 1989

often difficult to differentiate between the two, and that the real was often casually thrown in with the semiprecious.

Frames seem a likely way to finish a bag but here, even after the minuscule screws are fitted until they are flush, they aren't the final operation. Some bags have charms dangling, for no purpose other than to amuse. There are typewriters for businesswomen (computers soon?), telephones, airplanes, boats, and even, on occasion, the Statue of Liberty. The completed bags then go to a finisher who examines every part, buffs and polishes and sometimes, in the case of reptile skins, uses a blower to turn wrinkles into smooth, glossy surfaces.

Reptiles—alligator, lizard, karung snakeskin—are among the many types of skin that go into Leiber bags. Also used are calfskin and ostrich, suede, capeskin, and goat. Other skins, with even a remote possibility of success, have been tried, including fish skin, which, with one exception, didn't work. The exception is Swiss-finished "stingray" similar in appearance to Shagreen, the fine-grained sharkskin that was popular in the 1920s.

The minaudières, the metal evening bags for which Mrs. Leiber is particularly renowned—"truly magical" is how Rose Marie Bravo, president of Saks Fifth Avenue describes them—are created in two ways. The classic shapes are built out of cardboard and then sent to Italy where they are stamped in brass. On their return here, they are gold plated and get an English kidskin lining. Finally, the design is painted on, indicating the color of each section to be beaded.

Animal and more complex shapes begin with a sculpted wax model, which, in turn, is sent to Italy where it is copied, in part mechanically. Certain parts, which cannot be machine-copied—feet, ears—are cast separately and soldered on but done so finely that no seams are visible. Other parts—the head of a horse, the bow on a cat—are stamped in two halves and joined invisibly. The gold plating is done when the bags are returned to this country so that the thickness and quality of the plating can be controlled. Hinges, locks, and other hardware are put on in the workrooms here, again all by hand.

The beading of the bags began originally not as an artistic endeavor but as a matter of necessity. The plating on the first metal bags was so bad that some disguise was required, and Mrs. Leiber decided that covering the bag with crystals would both hide and enhance. The solution was so successful that even when the plating improved, there was no thought of returning to unadorned metal.

Although the rhinestone-encrusted evening bags require the most painstaking work as well as the most intensive labor, they are not the most difficult to manufacture. That honor, if such it be, belongs to bags made of real shells. First, there is the difficulty of finding suitable real shells and then, because like people, no two shells are alike, the frames have to be made to fit each one individually.

Add to this the fact that shells are fragile and that almost nothing can be done to toughen them up and, unsurprisingly, the result is that real shell bags are no longer among the Leiber designs.

Still, shells are a popular, and natural, handbag shape. Mrs. Leiber's solution was to design a metal bag, curved and undulating and although not the real thing, perhaps a cousin. She did some of them in unadorned gold and some, as might be expected, punctuated with jewels.

The solution, as well as it works, is not the final one in Mrs. Leiber's book. She is going to try the real thing again—and anyone familiar with her tenacity wouldn't quibble about odds.

White pearl and aurum stone egg,
drop-in chain, 1971

II

Precious Miniatures

Beverly Sills and Mary Tyler Moore show off their Judith Leiber eggs

Beverly Sills is, in her own words, "a great fan" of Judith Leiber. She is also a friend, a friendship that came about as a result of their respective talents.

They met in Milan when Ms. Sills was already an international name and was singing at La Scala Opera. Mrs. Leiber had long been an admirer and when she saw Ms. Sills sitting in what was then the Hotel Continentale, she went over and introduced herself. Later, in New York, Mrs. Leiber, as a tribute to an artist and to commemorate the meeting, sent her an evening bag. On her part, Ms. Sills, having learned of the Leibers' love of music, began inviting them to opera performances. In the intervening years, Ms. Sills has accumulated between fifty and sixty Leiber bags—"I've never counted them"—some gifts from Mrs. Leiber on special occasions, sent instead of a bouquet, but most of them either gifts from her husband, Peter Greenough, or gifts to herself. Among them are a number of the jeweled eggs, a lotus flower, several butterflies, and a glittery black and red mini-library that looks like a trio of books bound together.

"When people ask Judy what she does, she always says, 'I make bags,'" Ms. Sills said. "She doesn't. She is an incredible designer and her things are breathtakingly beautiful."

"I just love to hold them," she added. "I think she's an extraordinary artist."

One of Ms. Sills's favorite day bags, recently replaced when old age overtook it, was a specially designed tote, made to fit the dimensions of opera scores. Inside there was an additional little purse for makeup, essential when she was traveling constantly and meeting the press as soon as she stepped off the plane. The new tote is a similar design, in navy blue ostrich, but the opera scores have been replaced with board papers. Ms. Sills took over as chairman of Lincoln Center in early 1994.

Other fans of Mrs. Leiber both carry her bags and display them. Patricia Buckley, a grande dame of New York's social circuit, has a dozen or more bags, and one of them is usually on a table in her library. It's a gold metal dog, covered in brown and white crystals. It isn't a feature-for-feature copy of one of the Buckleys' three Cavalier dogs but, she said, "it's such a thing of beauty that it really doesn't matter."

"There's nothing like her bags, they are true works of art," Mrs. Buckley said. "I adore them."

Mrs. Buckley's collection includes a black and white grouse, a red and black ladybug, and a red, white, and blue American flag. The flag design, which she said, "everyone tries to steal," was a gift from Mrs. Leiber. It arrived when Mrs. Buckley, who had retained her Canadian citizenship for more than three decades, finally became an American citizen.

Mrs. Leiber's admirers leave few superlatives unturned when they talk about her and her creations. Mrs. Buckley's dog on display is modest compared to what some of them have come up with.

Katherine Rauch of Houston got her first Leiber bag when she was still living in Dallas and dating the banker who is now her husband. He had asked her to a ball, she couldn't make it, and as a substitute for the hoped-for evening together, he sent her a sparkling Leiber pumpkin. Since then, over the past twelve years, he has given her one on every special occasion, and she has added a few on her own. Now, between the leathers and the beaded, she has collected more than thirty.

Her "baby" bag—a jeweled metal bag that looks like a baby stretched out—is on a table in the living room; a frog design is on a foyer table. But most of her jeweled pieces are in a special display cabinet against one wall of her bath/dressing room.

Mrs. Rauch's display is not unique. But an action she took recently very likely is. She visited her attorney to draft her will and, along with some valuable pieces of art, she listed her jeweled Leiber bags.

The attorney was incredulous. "I'd like to ask one question," he said. "Do you mean that along with your art, you're going to will purses?" She affirmed that she was, indeed, going to do exactly that. "This is a first!" he said.

Mrs. Rauch has no doubts that the story has made the rounds in legal circles. But she's convinced that if he'd had any idea of what the bags looked like, he wouldn't have been as shocked.

"He didn't know about Judith Leiber," Mrs. Rauch said. "A lot of men don't."

Then again, a lot of men do. Many, hearing her name, say it is familiar to them and then do a double-take. "You cost me a lot of money," say some. Others say, she hopes in jest, "You're a troublemaker." She once said to one of them, "I hope you don't hate me," and he smiled: "Oh no, all I have to do is give one as a gift and I'm a hero."

There's a woman in the Midwest who owns dozens of Leiber bags, including the design based on the egg originally made by Carl Fabergé, the Russian court jeweler. The bag is a confection of pearls and rhinestones woven into ribbon-like bands and medallions. The bands of white pearls are inset with small sequined flowers and jeweled roses peek out from the medallions, all blazing from a bed of

Pat Buckley carries one of several Judith Leiber minaudières in her collection

ruby red. She also owns the bag that was the original Leiber minaudière. Mrs. Leiber calls it a chatelaine because it reminds her of the little purses once carried by the mistress of the castle to hold such essentials as scissors. A true, old-fashioned purse shape in gold metal, it is studded with a thick hem, a thin collar, and ribbons of rhinestones.

Back in 1975, Bernice Norman of New Orleans was in a dressing room at Bergdorf Goodman being outfitted for the season. Her special saleswoman brought in dresses she thought she'd like and another salesperson brought in accessories, including an evening bag made from an antique Japanese obi. The bag cost $800, which in those days was even more of a fortune than it is today.

"When I heard the price, I said, 'That's not to be believed—for a purse!'" Mrs. Norman said. "And the saleswoman said, 'I knew you were going to say that, but try it with the things you're looking at.'"

Once she did, Mrs. Norman said, she was "hooked, off and running, and the first thing I knew, I was looking for more Judith Leiber bags." She now has "close to three hundred," which is very likely something of a record.

She recently retired three big boxes containing about eighty bags that she hadn't worn for some time. "Put them to sleep for a bit," is how she described it. They're on a closet shelf and there they will stay until, eventually, her whole collection is given to a museum.

Part of the collection, about fifty handbags, has already had two museum exhibits. In 1986, the New Orleans Museum of Art's display of her Leiber bags attracted almost ten thousand people. The collection, in part or whole, can't be permanently donated to the museum because it doesn't have a costume section, she said, "but they're looking around for me."

"The purses are not only objects of great beauty but they show incredible craftsmanship," said John Bullard, the director, who suggested the show after seeing and admiring the bags at a number of parties.

After the New Orleans show, mounted as a show of art with some of the bags suspended on almost invisible wire and others laid in cases "like jewels," there was another request for it. The bags went on exhibit in a museum in Jackson, Mississippi.

Mrs. Norman keeps the bags she uses, more than two hundred of them, in drawers, each in its own flannel bag (she calls them "nightgowns"), stacked one against the other like slices of bread. Each "nightgown" has the top folded down so the handbag style can be identified.

Her favorite bag—an egg completely jeweled in a deep shade of pink and punctuated with small floral designs—sits on a stand on the coffee table in her living room. But it's not only a table *objet*—it is occasionally taken on an outing

Famed socialite Ann Bass bedecked in diamonds and a Judith Leiber minaudière

Multicolored butterfly, drop-in chain, 1982

*Ladybug in red, jet, and rhinestones, onyx dots
and lock, drop-in chain, 1989*

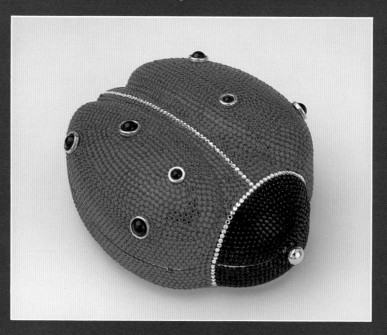

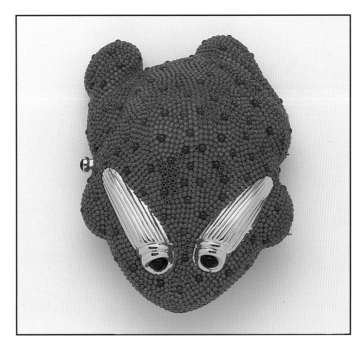

*Red rhinestone frog decorated with garnets,
drop-in chain, 1979*

Multicolored fantasy fish, drop-in chain, 1978

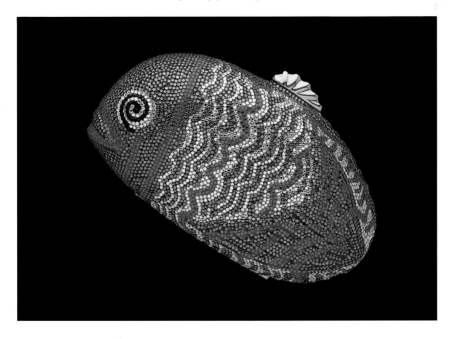

when a dress seems to call for it. Two other favorites, in addition to her original obi bag, are a pastel-shaded butterfly and a checkerboard oblong of emerald, ruby, amethyst, gold, and silver squares bordered in jet black.

Mrs. Norman's sister-in-law, Sunny Norman, who is active in the art world, is also a Leiber fan but a minor league one compared to her relative. She has "a couple of dozen" styles.

"I'm the bag lady," Bernice Norman says happily. "She's the art lady."

Although the New Orleans Museum has no appropriate place for the Norman bag collection, Leiber bags are, in fact, in the permanent collections of museums across the country, including the Smithsonian Institution in Washington, D.C., and the Chicago Historical Society. They are also to be seen in the Museum of Fine Arts, Houston, the Dallas Museum of Art, and the Los Angeles County Museum of Art.

The Costume Institute at the Metropolitan Museum of Art in New York is another prestigious institution that has recognized Mrs. Leiber's artistry.

"Judith Leiber's handbags both affirm and deny the handbag," says Richard Martin, the curator. "The soft bags suggest the luxury of materials. The hard bags become precious, referenced miniatures in the ways in which Joseph Cornell boxes become condensations of the most picturesque and evocative world."

The irony of the designs, Mr. Martin says, is that while they give women a place in which to cache the riches and remembrances of their lives, "the container becomes an even greater treasure than anything that could be held within."

At the Museum of the City of New York, JoAnne Olian describes Mrs. Leiber as "indisputedly the most important accessory designer of our time" but notes that the description is inadequate. "Her incomparable handbags and belts, executed in exotic skins, semiprecious stones, and anything else that strikes her fancy, truly merit the appellation of museum quality. She is a unique combination of artistry, wit, and *mittel* European practicality."

A number of the Leiber beaded bags are also scheduled for inclusion in a new gallery planned for the Art Museum of Western Virginia. The gallery will house the paintings, ivories, and other valuable art works of a prominent Roanoke family that has contributed several hundred thousand dollars for the project and considers the Leiber bags worthy of inclusion.

One tale, said not to be apocryphal and certainly a candidate for any "you think you've heard everything" contest, is of a husband who gave his wife fourteen Leiber bags in seven years and wanted them back as part of the divorce settlement. The wife refused. He reportedly snapped—with just a modicum of exaggeration—"I could retire on your Leiber bag collection."

Not quite, although one Leiber bag, made for an exhibit in collaboration

Whenever the stars come out, Leiber bags are bound to be spotted. Here, carrying their own Judith Leiber creations, are Joan Rivers (opposite, above), Lynda Carter (above), and Kathie Lee Gifford (with Joy Philbin, opposite, below)

with the jeweler Harry Winston, sold for almost $70,000 to a determined buyer who wouldn't accept that the bag wasn't designed for personal use. A pear-shaped box, fashioned of eighteen-karat gold, the bag had a gold lizard lining, a platinum collar set with diamonds, and a cabochon ruby clasp.

Considering the Leiber sales record, the fourteen bags in seven years wasn't anything near a record. Stores around the country report that multiple sales aren't unusual but the establishments that carry the handbags are usually upscale and prestigious—among them Saks Fifth Avenue, Bergdorf Goodman, Neiman-Marcus, Marshall Field, I. Magnin, Nordstrom—as well as a number of selected boutiques. The bags are also sold in London at Harvey Nichols, Asprey, Mappin & Webb, and Garrard. Two freestanding Leiber boutiques recently opened in Bangkok, Thailand, are the forerunners of planned jewel-box outlets in the Far East and Europe.

Despite the upscale purveyors, the twelve bags sold in a single purchase to a woman in Beverly Hills, and the fourteen to a woman in Oklahoma (who said she was too fat for clothes but could at least enjoy beautiful bags) aren't the norm. Nor is the woman who, whenever she chooses a bag, buys three of the style, one for each of her houses. As for the woman who buys four of most of her choices, one each for herself, her two daughters, and her daughter-in-law, even in the Leiber world, she's probably one of a kind.

More popular as multiple purchases are the Leiber small accessories. More than a few women—of obvious means—buy a dozen or more at a clip to use as favors at lunch or dinner parties. The pillboxes, many of them miniatures of the bags, are particular favorites at $180 each, and up, up, up. But there are as well such fripperies as minuscule notebooks, compacts, picture frames, card cases, and lipstick holders. Most of them are paved with rhinestones but there are also more tailored offerings inset with an inch or two of alligator skin, smooth leather, or soft calfskin.

The height of Leiber-inspired decorative ingenuity was undoubtedly that dreamed up by Patricia Moller of Los Angeles. Mrs. Moller invited eight of her women friends, who she knew had Leiber evening bags, and their husbands, to a dinner party. The women were asked to bring their Leiber bags. When they arrived, Mrs. Moller took all the bags (a few women brought more than one) and lined them up on a mirror, flanked with votive candles, running down the center of the dining table. The result was a centerpiece glowing with thousands of points of light. It is still being talked about and over the years the story has become a small decorating legend.

Mrs. Moller remembers it fondly. "It was gorgeous," she said. "They looked like jewels."

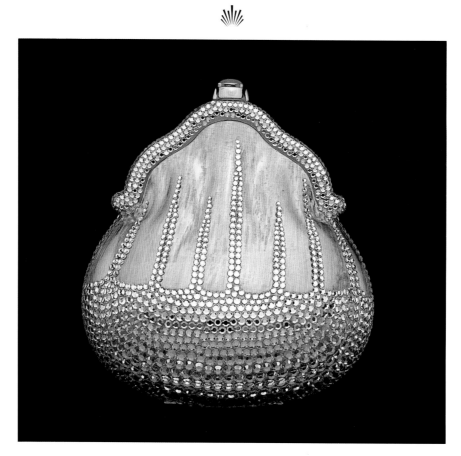

*Original version of the chatelaine
(Judith Leiber's first metal bag), 1967*

Earliest metal bag, the chatelaine, in gold/jet and silver/jet versions, all with drop-in chains, 1967

Group of geometric jet and rhinestone boxes. Clockwise from far left: octagon box, 1986; clover shaped box, 1989; oblong box with onyx and rhinestone trim, 1985; oval box with jet, rhine crisscross, and rhine center, 1992; oblong box with jet, rhinestone, and pearl decorations, 1973

Mrs. Moller, whose bag motto is "I find them, my husband buys them," said she considered Mrs. Leiber "the Fabergé of today—her bags are the art pieces of tomorrow, we all know that."

Andy Warhol also called them "art," although Mrs. Leiber says, with a chuckle that both affirms and denies the remark, "he was crazy." She also believes that he actually liked the bags better inside out but offers no proof for her conviction.

As for his description of her work as art, she shrugs it off. "Truthfully, I don't consider them art, I'm an artisan," she said.

Artist or artisan—she wasn't too happy when a New York painter took one of the designs and made it into a still life (although anyone that avant-garde possibly has another name for such a creation). The bag was, from all reports, glued to the canvas and then covered with paint. The obvious question is, if it's going to be covered with paint, why use a Leiber bag? and the answer could conceivably be that it was used for the same reason that women wear beautiful lingerie, even if no one else sees it. The person most concerned knows the quality hidden underneath.

Unless it's covered with paint (and probably even then), Mrs. Leiber has an unerring eye when it comes to spotting—or not spotting—her bags. When Barbara Walters first visited her showroom, the two enjoyed each other's company—but Barbara was not carrying a Leiber bag. When she was about to leave Mrs. Leiber said, tongue in cheek, "I listen to you on '60 Minutes.'" Barbara laughed: "You said that because I have a Chanel bag." Which was absolutely true. (Does it need to be explained that Miss Walters is not, nor has she ever been, on "60 Minutes?")

According to Ellin Saltzman, the fashion director of Bergdorf Goodman, there is even a Leiber admirer somewhere in the Paris underworld. Ms. Saltzman had checked her suitcase in Paris for a Concorde flight to London and was reading in the lounge when it was announced that the flight had been delayed due to fog. She made plans to return to her hotel, retrieved her case, and found that the lock had been shattered. Her favorite Leiber minaudière had been taken; another designer handbag was still there.

The Leiber customers have, over the years, included everyone from First Ladies to such celebrities as Joan Sutherland, Diana Ross, Claudette Colbert, and Mary Tyler Moore. Greta Garbo had one (whether or not she bought it herself is moot) as, apparently, does Queen Elizabeth. The British monarch was presented with a design Mrs. Leiber calls "a rounded square," completely beaded and finished with a sodalite stone lock, during her visit to California. The bag was a gift from Barbara Davis, wife of the oil and motion picture tycoon. Raisa Gorbachev has one too, presented by Barbara Bush.

Carol Petrie with a Leiber ladybug design

*Barbara Bush holding
a Judith Leiber day bag*

Mrs. Bush herself carried Leiber bags at several of the inaugural ceremonies after her husband's election. She wore a royal blue bag framed in marcasite to the inaugural ball, and an alligator bag for the swearing-in ceremony. She owns, as well, a dog bag, modeled after Millie, her springer spaniel. The metal animal fits into the palm of a hand, is encrusted with topaz, bronze, and clear rhinestones, has twinkling black onyx eyes, a tiny tongue, and a gold necklace. Duplicates of the design were sold at $2,500, and it is still popular because somehow the shape, the twinkle, and the tiny tongue translate to a remarkable resemblance to any number of canines.

Mrs. Bush's impeccable manners are remembered fondly by Mrs. Leiber and the staff. During her years in the White House, she visited the Leiber showroom, had her picture taken with the employees, and followed up by sending them autographed copies.

Nancy Reagan carried white satin Leiber bags at both of President Reagan's inaugural balls. The first was a small shirred clutch bag with a rock crystal scarab top closure, a rock crystal teardrop decorating the sides, and a silk shoulder strap. The bag for the second inaugural, a gathered envelope shape with a large rounded rhinestone ornament, was later sent back with a request that a coffee stain be removed; Mrs. Leiber made her another bag and kept the original. Mrs. Reagan also ordered a red lizard bag when she was preparing to accompany her husband to a European summit meeting. The personal call she made to place the order occasioned one of the more embarrassing moments in the Leiber business.

"Who is calling?" asked the young woman who was at the Leiber switchboard at the time.

"Mrs. Ronald Reagan calling for Mrs. Leiber," Mrs. Reagan replied.

"What company are you with?" was the next query.

Mrs. Reagan identified herself. Apparently the First Lady passed muster. She was put through.

The current First Lady, Hillary Rodham Clinton, has an evening bag modeled after Socks, the family cat, that was presented to her while she was still in Arkansas. The feline's body is of jet black and clear crystal rhinestones, the paws are white chalk stones, and there's a perky rhinestone bow.

Special orders are a minute percentage of the Leiber business but some requests can't be resisted. One was executed for a patriotic Texan invited to the Clinton inauguration. It has the Stars and Stripes on one side and the Statue of Liberty on the other. Don't ask the price.

Mrs. Leiber's newest patriotic bag is a whimsical "Fourth of July tomato." It's round and red, naturally, and punctuated on one side with a blue segment and a crystal star—definitely not for barbecue or picnic. And she's still fond of her

*White satin evening envelope with rhinestone ornament, original bag
made for Nancy Reagan for her inaugural gown, 1984*

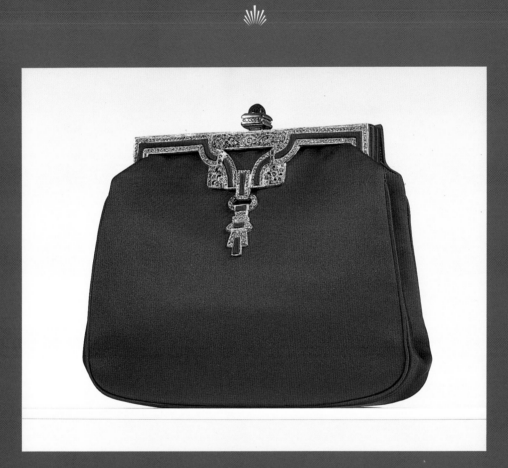

*Royal blue satin evening clutch, duplicate of bag made for the inaugural gown
of Barbara Bush (original in the Smithsonian Institution), 1988*

"Peace" bag, designed after the Gulf War but one that she likes to think has some meaning at all times. The bag, in the shape of a dove, has "Peace" in English, French, Hebrew, and Arabic, spelled out in varied-hued rhinestones.

Peace dove bag, multihued rhinestones, drop-in chain, 1991

Mrs. Leiber has been honored not only by the women, known and unknown, who value her creativity but by her peers in the fashion business. Her first important recognition came after she had been in business only six years. She was given the Swarovski Great Designer award for artistic use of the company's rhinestones and crystals. Since then, she has received most of the industry's major awards including the Council of Fashion Designers Award for Accessories in 1994 and, in 1991, the Silver Slipper Award of the Costume Institute of the Museum of Fine Arts, Houston. She was also the first in her field to be given a Coty Fashion Award (1973) and in 1980 was awarded the Neiman-Marcus Winged Statue for Excellence in Design. In 1993, she was given an honorary degree of Doctor of Fine Arts by the International Fine Arts College in Miami.

On occasion, she makes personal appearances at stores, preferably if they can be worked in with another event—an honor she is about to receive or a personal visit. She is usually somewhat of a surprise to the customers who come to meet her for the first time, and to the women who have just heard of her.

The initial surprise stems from the fact that although she is an extraordinarily sophisticated woman, she leaves anything but that impression. In truth, she looks motherly—motherly in the way mothers used to look—or like a favorite aunt. This adds up to salt and pepper hair, eyes with a glint of mischief lurking in them, a ready smile, a deep, resonant voice, and a warm personality. There is no sleekness and none of the artifice associated with the fashion business. She has a genuine—and sometimes wicked—sense of humor and a sincere interest in the person to whom she's talking. If there's no interest, there's also no pretense.

There is, too, as with mothers and favorite aunts, a getting-down-to-basics decisiveness. In her case, at the personal appearances, it's what she can learn from customers, what they want, and what they may particularly like or perhaps dislike. And it's selling—how much she can sell and how she can help the salespeople sell both immediately and in the future.

A few years ago, a reporter for *The New Yorker* stayed with her at a Saks Fifth Avenue in-store appearance and related a couple of her *bon mots*. Included was one of her favorite answers when she's asked what kind of handbag she carries. "One of my own, of course," she says, giving an "I can't believe this" look. "Either that or a paper bag and I won't carry a paper bag so you figure it out."

Another exchange, original with the *New Yorker* report, was of a husband who told Mrs. Leiber that he had long been an admirer of hers. "Actually my wife more than me," he said. "That's good," she said, "you shouldn't be carrying handbags, you aren't the type." In the words of the magazine: "could you die?"

The most telling exchange of the afternoon was between Mrs. Leiber and a saleswoman who was holding a customer's credit card and a bag shaped like a pig. The saleswoman wondered if the pig should be sold. It was, after all, a sample.

"Darling, please. Don't give me a heart attack," Mrs. Leiber said. "Sell the pig. There's more where that came from."

Oblong suede envelope with collapsible handle, semiprecious stone and rhinestone decorated lock, 1991

III

The Bag Lady from Budapest

The handbag business wasn't an option that Judith Peto considered when she was growing up in Budapest. Her parents were well-to-do and not too different from the middle-class norm in those days. Her father, Emil Peto, whose roots were Austro-Hungarian, was in charge of a grain department in a bank. Later, he went into the jewelry business and employed a staff of salesmen to travel throughout the country. Her Viennese mother, Helen, stayed home, and her older sister, Eva, seemed content to follow her mother's footsteps.

The lifestyle of her mother and sister was never even considered for "Judy." Her parents had other plans for the high-spirited, always-in-motion younger daughter. They had decided that she would become a chemist. There was some—but not much—logic to the decision. It was based on the fact that her mother's cousin in Romania had developed a popular complexion cream and made a fortune. If the cousin could do it, young Judy, strong-willed and extremely intelligent, could most certainly do it as well.

Mrs. Leiber looks back on it now with some incredulity. "I thought the idea was full of soup," she said, using one of the many slightly strange phrases that seem to be original with her. "But I was very much under my mother's thumb—can you believe that even in my late teens, my mother and sister picked all my clothes?"

As the first step in what was planned as a cosmetic queen's future, she was sent to England. There, later that same year, she was scheduled to enroll at one of the great universities and pursue the scientific studies that would lead to the fortune. It wasn't to be. Before the fall semester began, she returned to Budapest to see her family. The year was 1939. The month she should have been en route back to England, World War II began. The theoretical cosmetics empire vanished, never to be seriously considered again.

"Hitler put me in the handbag business," Mrs. Leiber now says, because it was only when the Nazis began rolling through Europe that the possibility of making handbags began to seem, if not ideal, at least not unattractive. Handbags had always seemed appealing. Her mother had always loved them and her father had always enjoyed buying beautiful designs as gifts for his wife, scouting the best shops throughout Europe during his business travels.

There were, as well, other reasons for the career switch. A peripheral one was an intelligence test she had taken that had indicated an exceptionally strong

Black patent leather accordion gusseted flap envelope with slender handles, 1963. From the collection of Eva Ecker

sense of color. But the crucial reason was that the Petos were Jewish, and in the 1930s and 1940s, the artisan guilds in Hungary were open to Jews while professional opportunities for Jews were severely limited.

"There was a stricture against Jews, mostly to keep us out of important positions and upper classes things," Mrs. Leiber said. "Making handbags was not considered very upper class."

She was, as she puts it, "the first woman with enough *chutzpah* to apply to the Guild," and for reasons she never knew and never questioned, she was immediately accepted. Her training began with sweeping the floor and cooking the glue.

While she was learning her craft, the Nazi war machine was cutting a wide swath, invading country after country. Trains were carrying millions of Jews to concentration camps. For some time, Hungary was relatively safe. However, after it was invaded, hundreds of thousands of Jews who lived in rural areas were rounded up while those in Budapest faced increasing harassment. The Soviet army was approaching Budapest from the east and despite the Nazis' knowledge that the end was near, they were determined to continue, as long as possible, their mission to exterminate the Jews. Ghettos were established, executions took place, and forced marches began.

It was during this period when the administration was breaking down that the Nazis began bartering some Jewish lives for needed supplies. It was also the time when Raoul Wallenberg, the Swedish diplomat who saved the lives of thousands of Jews, was active in the area.

A small quirk of fate spared the Peto sisters as other Jewish women were rounded up for camps and death. They had been given a job mending pants at the Jewish Community House, and as this was considered vital to the war effort, they were allowed to continue. But mending pants wasn't enough to save the family. That was accomplished by a Hungarian employee of the Swiss legation, the relative of a family friend, who arranged for the Swiss to issue a "Schutz" pass to Mr. Peto. The pass was essential, in effect guaranteeing the bearer's safety. Once it was in Mr. Peto's possession, it underwent a degree of creative forgery. It was changed so that it became valid for the whole family rather than for just an individual.

The war was still on when Mrs. Leiber completed her Guild training, and although she then had the skills, there was no place to use them. As with many novice entrepreneurs, she began working at home, making handbags out of whatever materials she could lay her hands on. When some of the essentials weren't available, she merely added a dollop of ingenuity, including drapery trim.

"I'm the product of an archaic European system where you learned your craft from the bottom up," she says. "I like to know how to do things from start

Not all of Judith Leiber's minaudières are made of hard metal.
This "Peacock"-patterned soft minaudière in the collection of
The Metropolitan Museum of Art, New York, dates from 1979

Pinto bean-shaped minaudière, drop-in chain, 1994

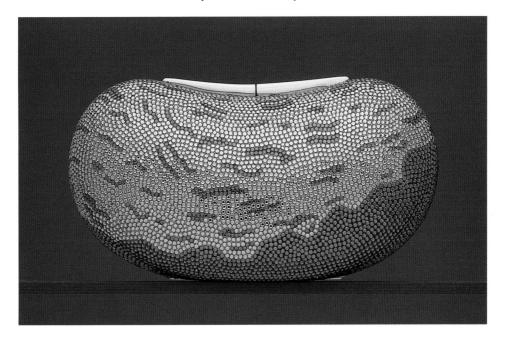

to finish. I was first an apprentice, then a journeyman, and finally a master. By the time you're a master, you've been through all the stages of making a handbag, from cutting and sewing to framing, adding handtacks, and polishing."

There is no operation in her present business with which she isn't thoroughly familiar and which she is not able to do herself. "Every tiny detail that there is, I've done myself, from plating the skin of an Indonesian karung snake to beading," she said. She no longer skives leather (thinning it at the edges to make it more malleable) or glazes reptile skins to a mirror shine with a piece of hot agate—but she hasn't forgotten how.

As thorough as the Guild training was, it missed one aspect for future entrepreneurs. It was designed to turn out first-class craftsmen, not businessmen. That area, which later became essential to her, was taken in hand by her father.

"He taught me the basics of business," she said. Later, when she owned her own business in New York, her father, at his own request, worked for her and came in daily until he was in his eighties. "I used to give him money for taxis and one day he fell on the street and I discovered he was taking the bus," she said. "I thought it was time for him to stop—I knew I could never trust him to take taxis."

Life for everyone in Hungary began changing in 1945. For Judith Peto, the future arrived in the person of Gerson Leiber, a Signal Corps sergeant in the United States Army, who landed in Budapest after trekking across Algiers and Italy. (He has always thought he was assigned to the Signal Corps because he kept pigeons—he still thinks so and he still keeps pigeons.) He was with a friend searching for quarters and she was with a friend on the street outside her building, not doing much of anything. But, she insists, she did not talk to him until her friend had exchanged some banter with the two soldiers, and "more or less" made impromptu and informal introductions.

The encounter still merits a smile. "I was attracted to him but I was brought up not to speak to strangers," she says, breaking into a wide grin. "I let my friend do the dirty work and I reaped the benefits."

Mr. Leiber's memory is equally vivid. It was his second day in Budapest and, he said, "I saw the girl of my dreams, it was love at first sight."

The two young people both loved art and spent whatever free time they had roaming through museums. Her at-home business also took an upturn. After enlisting two State Department secretaries to act as part-time sales agents, she began making handbags for women in the American legation (and most importantly, was paid in sought-after dollars). He began studying painting at the Royal Academy in Budapest and sending some of his finished work home. His mother burned the nudes. He just painted more.

Mr. Leiber, an abstract expressionist, is a member of the National Academy of Design and has paintings hanging in many private collections, as well as the permanent collection of the Art Students League of New York. He also has prints in museums around the world, including the Philadelphia Museum of Art, the Smithsonian Institution, the Victoria and Albert in London, the Dublin Gallery of Art, the Malmo Museum in Sweden, and the Israel Museum in Jerusalem.

The Leibers were married in 1946 and left Budapest the following year, she a G.I. bride returning with her husband to the city of his birth (Mr. Leiber was born in Brooklyn).

Her first encounter with America was, not surprisingly, an immigration officer. Somewhat more surprisingly, this immigration officer was also a fashion critic.

"I was wearing a pair of white felt waterproof boots when I came off the ship," she said. "The officer looked at me like I was a crazy person. He asked me where I thought I was going, there was no snow here. I felt terrible."

Exit one pair of white felt boots. She still thinks about them on cold days, with a touch of nostalgia but no regrets. Her footwear now has progressed beyond white felt—it can pass muster with the sharpest fashion eyes. As can her wardrobe, made up primarily of designs by Geoffrey Beene and Giorgio Armani, both of whom have an imagination and passion for perfection similar to her own.

The young bride ditched her boots and went to work almost simultaneously. The work was a job the union got her, in a concern that made cheap handbags. She knew it wasn't for her from the moment she walked in the door, but there was no alternative.

"The owner said to me, 'you remember how you made bags in Hungary, all the hand work, well, that's not how we do it here. Here we bake them like strudel in sheets.'" When the work was done and the bag finished, it was thrown into a bin that looked like a laundry basket. "I was used to handling each bag like a baby and I couldn't stand it," she said.

She escaped the strudel assembly line, went on to several other firms which manufactured better quality bags, and finally to a job with a firm known for fine handbags. There, Mrs. Leiber's talent was recognized with successive promotions and she stayed on, happily, for fourteen years, until the American operation was closed.

It was then that Mr. Leiber stepped in, with a firm foot. "You're not going to work for anybody anymore," he told her. "We're going to try it on our own." She was scared but willing. She says of her designing, "If it doesn't work right away, I don't pursue it," and the same attitude applied to the business. Its success was gradual, but never in doubt.

That was in 1963. The two rented a loft, so small that they sometimes thought they were working in a bedroom. The loft was in an old building with a rickety elevator that held only three people and shut down on weekends. The two-day closure, to people just starting a business and working seven days a week, meant walking up seven flights, even then an exercise they did not appreciate. There were six employees and one-third of them were named Leiber.

The one thing about which Mrs. Leiber had no doubts was the kind of bags she was going to produce. "I knew right from the beginning what I was going to do," she said. "I was going to make the best. I hate junk. The vision of what I'm doing today was there then."

Mr. Leiber was an active part of the business from the beginning. He had an official title, vice-president/treasurer, but his unofficial one was even more integral to the business.

"Because of his art background, Gus has always been the major critic of my designs," Mrs. Leiber said. "He has input in the coloring of the leather and the shapes and proportions of the bags. He's more classic and I'm more ornate in taste and it's wonderful to bounce around ideas with him."

At one time, one of his paintings provided a design inspiration. The painting, *The Cocktail Party*—a man hovering over a somewhat sultry woman holding a cocktail glass—was priced at $10,000. The handbag, with the figures and cocktail glass paved in rhinestones, was priced at $3,500. Both sold.

Mr. Leiber does not downplay the role he has played in the business. But the question he's most often asked has nothing to do with his contributions. What the questioners, interviewers, and others generally want to know is how two people who have been so closely involved in business for so many years have managed to avoid major disagreements. The answer to the question is that the premise isn't valid—they haven't avoided disagreements, major or minor. They compromise and work them through. Mr. Leiber occasionally opts for another answer, said only partly in jest. "The secret is letting her do what she wants to do." She rolls her eyes a little and sloughs off the remark. "Yeah!" she says.

On a more personal level—as it relates to the business—he is an important stabilizing influence for a woman whose stability is seasoned with more than a pinch of volatility. He often turns her complaints into laughter and brings her back to reality when she expects, and demands, constant perfection.

"When I do something like complain about circles under my eyes, he'll say to me, 'Judy, in your business you should have bags,' and of course I laugh and forget the circles," she said. "And he's a calming voice about things I can't change."

Minaudière inspired by Gerson Leiber painting, drop-in chain, 1992

Minaudière inspired by Faith Ringgold quilt, THE STREET, *drop-in chain, 1981.*
From the collection of Bernice Steinbaum

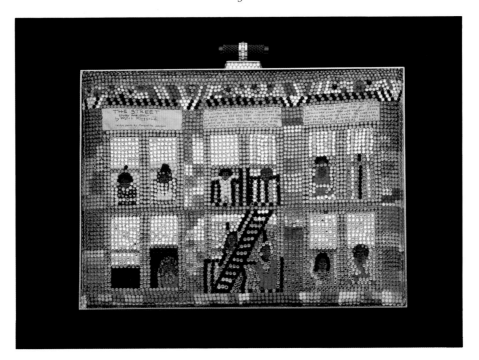

To everyone's surprise including, to a degree, their own, the Leibers finally, after many offers, sold their company in 1993. The buyer was Time Products, a British firm that distributes the designs of some of the world's most prestigious watch makers.

Mrs. Leiber, who remains as president and designer, said she accepted this offer, after refusing others, because she wanted the business to continue after she leaves, "but I'll work until I die and we're a long-lived family," she said. There were other reasons too: the offer came from Marcus Margulies, a man with similar ideas about quality, style, and luxury. The world-wide expansion, which he envisions eventually encompassing other luxury products, was always Leiber's dream; in this way it could be realized. There are already the two freestanding boutiques in Bangkok and others are in the planning stages.

Mr. Leiber, who left the business when it was sold, is now back as a consultant, at his wife's request. "I didn't realize how much I would miss his ideas and how much he contributed," she said.

Since the sale of the business, Mrs. Leiber has not trimmed her ten-to-twelve-hour work day; rather, she said, she is busier than ever. She is almost always on hand—somewhere on the showroom floor or the brightly lit workrooms beneath it—when her employees arrive and when they leave.

The Leibers have an eight-room triplex in Manhattan, three blocks from her place of business, a seven-room house in Easthampton that they bought in 1956, and a Norwich terrier named Sterling.

The Easthampton house is done in a style that can only be described as "sink-into comfort." It is almost the antithesis of Mrs. Leiber's sophisticated professional approach. There are antiques, paintings, sculptures, and hundreds of books but the house is the product of catholic taste and four decades of eclectic accumulation. It has, like its owners, aged without artifice.

It is, as well, the antithesis of the extensive gardens, once described as leaving a first impression of a "little Tuileries." In fact, the gardens are impressive but not grand, a marriage planned by Mr. Leiber of country simplicity and old-world formality. A passionate gardener, he has, over the years, continually added to the garden's acreage beginning with no specific plan but, like a painting, "working at it until something comes out." Particularly concerned with proportion, he has designed and cultivated, with help, a grape arbor, evergreens, plants, flowers, brick paths, courtyards, hedges, and trellises, each in a space specifically chosen to blend happily with the neighboring growth.

The Manhattan triplex is a blend of city and country, old and new. There is an enclosed plant-strewn dining terrace overlooking Park Avenue and a small, imaginatively planted conservatory at the opposite end. A former maid's room, situated over the small but modern kitchen, serves as Mrs. Leiber's study, used primarily as an at-home design studio.

The living room features an impressive display of antique Chinese blue and white porcelain, Egyptian and Roman sculptures, seventeenth-century bronzes, and works by Henry Moore, Constantino Nivolo, and Jacques Lipshitz. Cushions made of antique tapestries are strewn on sofas and chairs. Most of the walls have one or more examples of Mr. Leiber's work.

The Leibers have a houseman to look after the apartment, hired when Mrs. Leiber first began putting in her twelve-hour days. They are without help in the Easthampton house, where Mrs. Leiber does the cooking, Mr. Leiber does a good deal of the gardening, and both get most of their reading—and relaxing—done.

Ebony box carved in India, hardware made in Italy, carnelian stone, 1978

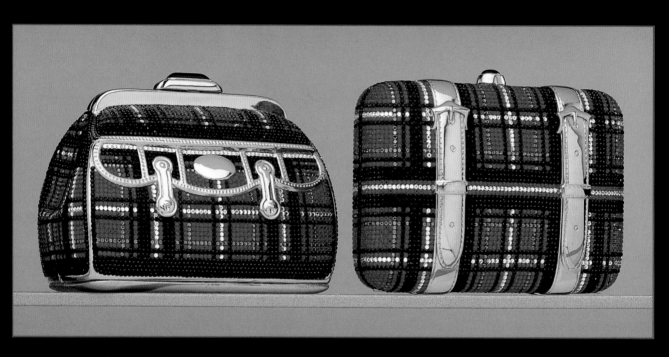

Left: red and black tartan patterned satchel, 1992. Right: black and red tartan patterned suitcase, 1989

IV

Handbags Through the Ages

More than half a century ago, the late Diana Vreeland, the legendary high priestess of fashion, using the royal "we," announced that "we're going to eliminate all handbags." At the time, she had a shirt with inside, rather than outside pockets, and carried in them lipstick, rouge, powder, comb, cigarettes, and money. It might be difficult to understand how she could distribute all these items in inside pockets without little bumps and lumps showing through her clothes but ours is not to reason—or question. She said she did. Therefore, she asked rhetorically, why in the world would she need a "bloody old handbag"?

Mrs. Vreeland was not the most practical woman, which undoubtedly contributed to her extraordinary sense of fashion, but as she might possibly have admitted, abolishing, exiling, writing off the handbag was not her most brilliant dictum. It perhaps rated only slightly above the idea of polishing the soles of shoes, which she was said to have done in her personal wardrobe.

Needless to say, the answer to her handbag question didn't take too long in coming. Mrs. Vreeland never did do away with the handbag, even on a personal basis, and most women don't even think about it. They know, as they have for some six centuries that, to one degree or another a handbag, if not absolutely necessary, is at least a convenience. It is, indeed, possible to stuff a few things in a few pockets but "few" is the operative word, and even carrying a minimal amount in that manner detracts from a sleek silhouette.

True, in earlier years, it was the gallant thing for men to carry the follies that women thought necessary to their well-being when they ventured outside their homes. And when it came to royalty and the rich, there were ladies-in-waiting and servants who followed them around, holding anything that would spoil the effect of their carefully considered silhouettes. Today, the bagless are still the exceedingly rich or royalty, although the bagless royalty is apt to be from some exotic land. The more down-to-earth variety of royal—Queen Elizabeth, for example—usually carry a fairly sturdy, good-sized handbag, of no observable style or distinction, and it is generally hooked on the left arm. A shoulder bag on a royal is a rare sight.

The women who are able to do without handbags, and there are a few, manage to get through their day with only a lipstick, tiny mirror, and credit card in a pocket—but they have a secret. It's immediately outside wherever they alight. There is a car and driver awaiting their pleasure, the car used not only for trans-

Tubular frame pouch with fold-down handles in red calfskin, 1978

portation but as a boudoir to hold makeup, notes, portable phone, books, and other paraphernalia necessary to modern life. The same paraphernalia that, not so incidentally, goes into the handbag of the vast majority of women.

When the early handbags and purses evolved, life was simpler and there was considerably less to carry. The names—"handbag" and "purse"—stem from the Latin *bursa* and the Greek *byrsa,* meaning bag and hide, and denote a pouch that was generally attached to a belt. For some years, this pouch was apparently worn solely by men as a receptacle for coins, the only currency at the time.

The name "pocketbook" came later, first surfacing in 1617 and denoting a small book of addresses or notes that fit in a pocket. By 1816, according to William Safire, the language maven, women were carrying a booklike case with compartments for papers and knickknacks, and they called it a purse, a handbag or—extending the old term—a pocketbook. Somehow the old term is still quite widely used in the United States, although it is rarely heard in other English-speaking countries such as England and Canada.

Among the early bags were those crafted by artisans of the leather workers guild in twelfth-century Florence. They were known not only for simple leather bags but more ornate ones, some decorated with jewels, some with gold, and the most elaborate with both jewels and gold. Fine silk bags were made in Venice. The bags were designed for and used primarily by men. By the sixteenth century, men's bags had become smaller (reportedly because the men also had to carry weapons) and in the seventeenth century bags for men virtually disappeared when wide breeches, which allowed for concealed pockets, came into fashion. In the centuries that followed, bags for men appeared and disappeared intermittently.

Women apparently were slower to appreciate the unique qualities of the handbag, adopting the idea sometime after the men. They also had less need for them, because of servants and men carrying their essentials. However, during the Renaissance, women frequently tied two drawstring bags to their belts. By the sixteenth century, a man often gave his fiancee a purse of velvet, silk, or leather containing portraits of the couple fashioned in enamel, gems, and gold. Even earlier, the Normans had what they called an *aulmonière,* the name derived from the same root as alms and almoner. The pouch or purse was suspended from a girdle by long laces of silk or gold.

By the eighteenth century, women's purses were flat and oblong, many with a loop attached to a belt. Still, despite the availability of bags and a fashion era that featured pockets concealed inside the panniers of dresses, it was servants who often carried in their own voluminous pockets the necessities required by their mistresses. This historical tidbit could have been where Mrs. Vreeland got

Red and rhine bulls-eye box, drop-in chain, 1987

*Tiny box inspired by a bunch of coins knotted into a Provençal
kerchief, red ground, jet and rhinestone decoration, 1987*

the idea of carrying her necessities in inside pockets, but Mrs. Vreeland—and her readers—did not often have dresses with panniers.

A century later, the favored silhouette was close-fitting and the absence of pockets once again encouraged the use of a handbag. The game bags used to hold catches of game and fish inspired one of the styles about this time; it was known as a *gibeciere* and chained in gold or silver.

However, this was a period when a number of other shapes and styles also emerged. Small bags, which hung from cords or chains and swung almost to the knees, were known as "balantines." A number of medium sized bags were urn-shaped and had long handles of materials that allowed wrapping around wrist or waist and some were designed in floral and shell shapes. In France, after the revolution, the *réticule,* usually a drawstring design with short silk handles carried on the arm, became popular. Envelope-shaped flat bags in soft leather, sometimes fringed on three sides, were also frequently seen.

Still, it wasn't until the latter part of the nineteenth century that some of the more noteworthy designs and ideas came into being. Among them were short-handled and small bags, rounded, octagonal, and shell shaped. These were made in materials that ranged from velvet and silk stretched over embossed cardboard to lace interwoven with gold and silver thread and hand-painted linens and lace.

The twentieth century marked the progress of the handbag from individual craftsmen-produced articles to mass market manufactured accessories. It also marked the time when women's attitudes and lives changed markedly. The less restrictive corsets that were introduced in the early part of the century and the advent of World War I, with great numbers of women working on assembly lines, both led to a feeling of greater freedom. The handbag became indispensable to thousands who were having their first work experience outside the home. Small bags gave way to large utilitarian styles with zippers and outside pockets, meant to carry a good deal more that earlier designs.

The early part of the twentieth century also saw the introduction of the minaudière, a gilded metal box, originally flat but soon to be seen in many shapes. Although metal and jeweled cases and boxes had long been popular as ornaments and for use in a boudoir, the minaudière, as we know it now, is said to have been the brainchild of Charles Arpels of the famed jewelry house of Van Cleef & Arpels. The story is that he had seen Florence Gould, wife of an American railroad magnate, using a metal cigarette box to carry her lipstick, cigarettes, and lighter. He decided to make a more luxurious version for evening wear, somewhat but not a great deal larger. The name "minaudière" apparently came from Alfred Van Cleef; a somewhat loose but popularly accepted translation is "coquettish air."

Lizard tailored frame clutch with sculptured leather inlaid handle, 1990

The variety of handbags available in the last few decades is almost beyond imagination, powered both by need and by their acceptance as an accessory that contributes to an overall fashion statement. For some years, the status bags (still considered so by some) were those emblazoned with designer names or initials on the fabric, leather, or clasp. More recently, status has become signatures that don't show themselves, small inside plaques hidden to outside view, the designer or prestigious maker recognizable only by intangibles in design and quality. A good percentage of the handbags sold today are at least inspired by these status designs, both those with obvious identification and those of a more discrete nature. Many more are outright copies and copies of copies, a hydra-headed monster that despite customs interceptions and lawsuits, has not yet been completely killed off.

There are few shapes still unexplored, few materials not yet used, and few sizes as yet untried. And each shape, size, and material, melded together, tells its own story. Almost all of them provide not-so-small clues to the personality, occupation, and even financial status of the woman carrying them. The young and funky, and even the not-so-young and funky, usually consider unobtrusive little clutches, discrete envelopes, vanity cases, and modest box-shapes akin to foreign objects. On the other hand, it might be said that there are few establishment arms attached to laundry-sized totes, enormous satchels, and fringed pouches.

It might be said but that's a yes and no and not exactly. The situations still generally apply but it's becoming increasingly difficult to deduce age and attitude—even by handbag. Women at every level of the workplace account for this rattling, confusing, and to some, upsetting change. Who in earlier years would have pegged as an executive the woman with an exaggerated tote or squashy duffle? And who, at one time, would have thought the young woman with the small alligator bag a junior secretary who believes in quality?

There is only one current certainty. With due respect to the late fashion doyenne, the fact is that the handbag is unlikely to disappear anytime soon.

DAY BAGS

*Yellow alligator frame bag with double bow closing,
semiprecious stones, and drop-in shoulder strap, 1980*

*Brown alligator pleated clutch on ridged
gate frame, 1980*

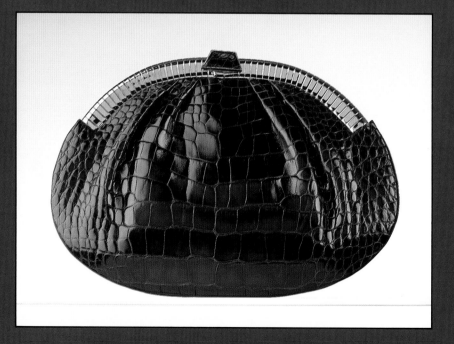

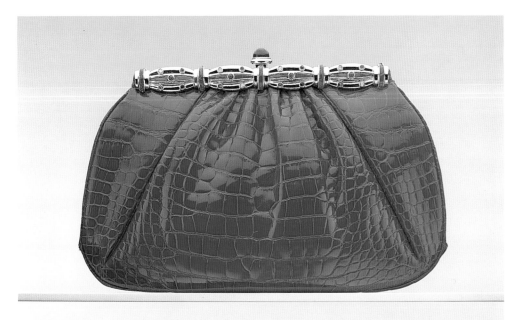

*Purple shirred alligator frame clutch with semiprecious
stone decoration, 1992*

*Small frame bag with special pull-down lock
with semiprecious stones, 1990*

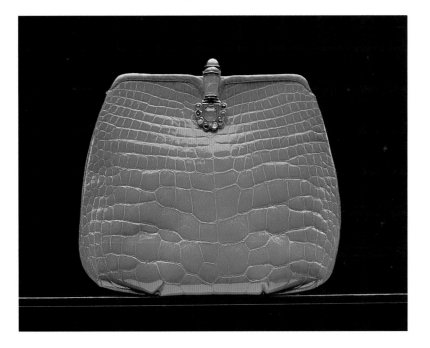

*Rounded envelope in light green alligator with chain
shoulder strap with medallions, 1989*

Triple entry shoulder bag, black calf and caramel
alligator combination, 1992

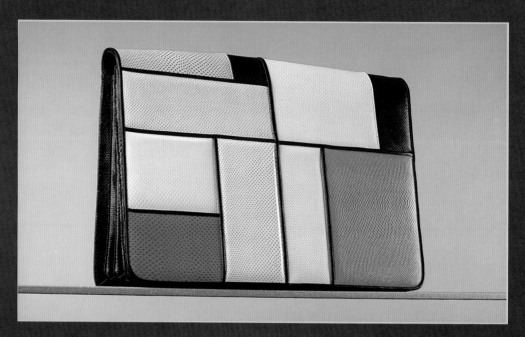

Envelope inspired by Piet Mondrian painting, 1990

Envelope inspired by Georges Braque painting, 1990.
From the collection of Agnes Gund

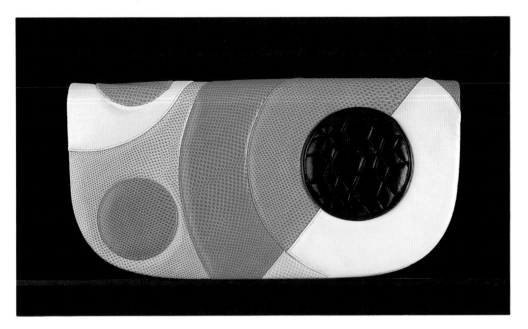

Envelope inspired by Sonia Delaunay painting, 1990

Geometric patterned envelope of ostrich, alligator, and calf, 1987

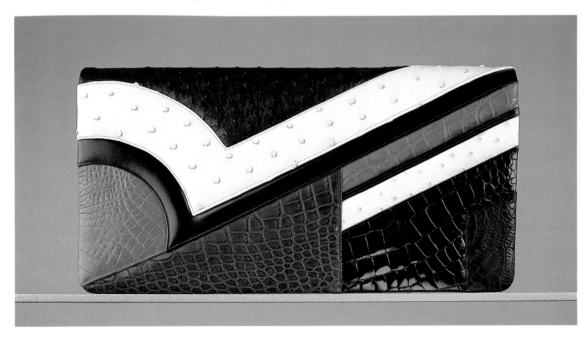

Bauhaus-inspired envelope of suede, calf, and patent, 1973.
From the collection of Eva Ecker

Art Deco envelope of black snake, black lizard, metallic python,
rhinestone trimmed, 1973

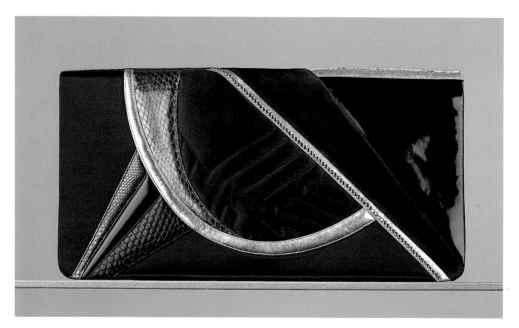

Karung snake envelope with multicolor stripes on cover and multicolor gussets, 1989

*Three "007" bags with special compartments. Small size with cord handle, 1990;
two larger ones with rigid top handles, 1993*

*Yellow, orange, and green mini-shoulder bags, one with American Indian style ornament,
two with bow ornaments, 1992*

*Tubular gold- and silver-plated bar with semiprecious
stone lock on blue karung, 1987*

*Green karung frame clutch with flower basket lock decorated
with semiprecious stones, 1989*

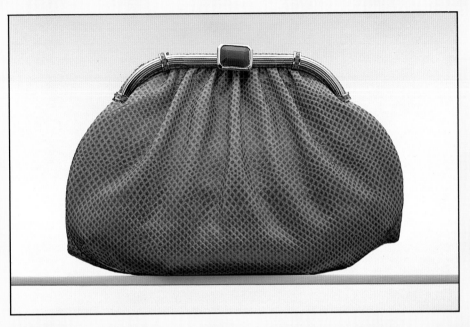

Tubular gold and silver frame on light green karung snake pouch, 1987

Multistone decorated curved frame pouch, 1994

Gold ring lizard box bag with silk cord shoulder handle, 1993

Bright green python box bag with sculptured gold hardware
and rigid handle, 1966

Nail head embroidered over white calf suitcase, 1969

Karung leather inlaid florentined box with shaped top handle, 1968.
From the collection of Margay Lindsey

Top right:
Brown calf bag with rigid handle and watch fob
(Collection The Metropolitan Museum of Art, New York), 1969

Bottom right:
Green ostrich envelope with rigid top handle, 1989. Black alligator bag of this style
worn by Mrs. Bush at President Bush's inauguration ceremony

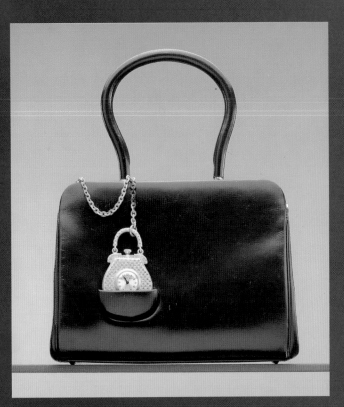

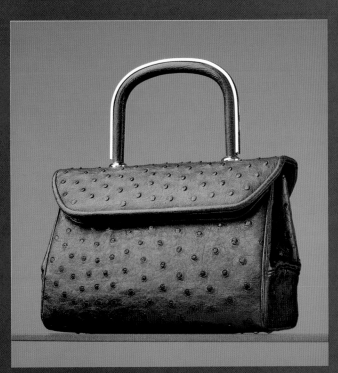

*Zebra-inspired frame tote with zebra enameled
circular handles, 1991*

*Two leopard-pattern quilted bags, one with circular leopard handles,
enamel, and semiprecious stone decoration, 1991*

Small cape clutch, studded with nailheads on brown patent leather,
inlaid gate frame with detachable chain handle, 1966

Orange and chalk embroidered over orange capeskin
suitcase bag, 1990

Emerald karung gathered frame pouch with varicolored
semiprecious stones on lock, 1993

Green pleated karung snake frame pouch with emerald
and clear rhinestone decorated carnation, 1993

*Purple karung frame clutch with undulating metal bar
and semiprecious lock, 1985*

*Clover lock with semiprecious stones on forest
green gathered alligator pouch, 1989*

Eyelet embroidered clutch with leather tassel in black karung snake, 1992

Nailhead embroidery on black satin clutch, 1972

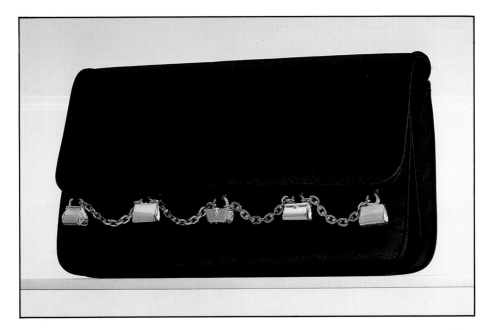

Black silk envelope with tiny bags hanging from chain on flap, 1994

Black karung snake envelope with chain decoration of pendants expressing world travel, 1990

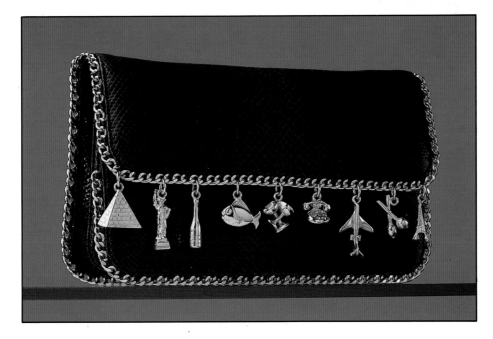

*Four "boroso" envelopes in red, purple, black, and navy, made of sharkskin
with matching karung trim, 1990*

Black satin and suede woven envelope trimmed in satin, 1978

*African hand-embroidered kinte cloth facile frame tote
with karung snake trim, 1976*

Tiny frame bag made of Indian hand embroidery with gold kid decoration
(Collection The Metropolitan Museum of Art, New York), 1973

Triple zipper pouches made of Afghan embroidery trimmed in black satin
(Collection The Metropolitan Museum of Art, New York), 1978

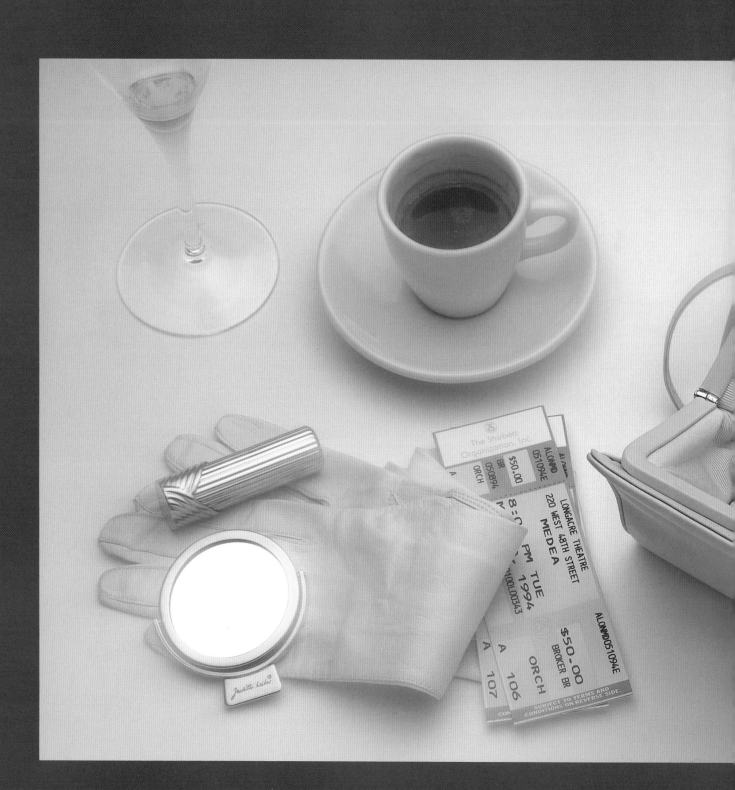

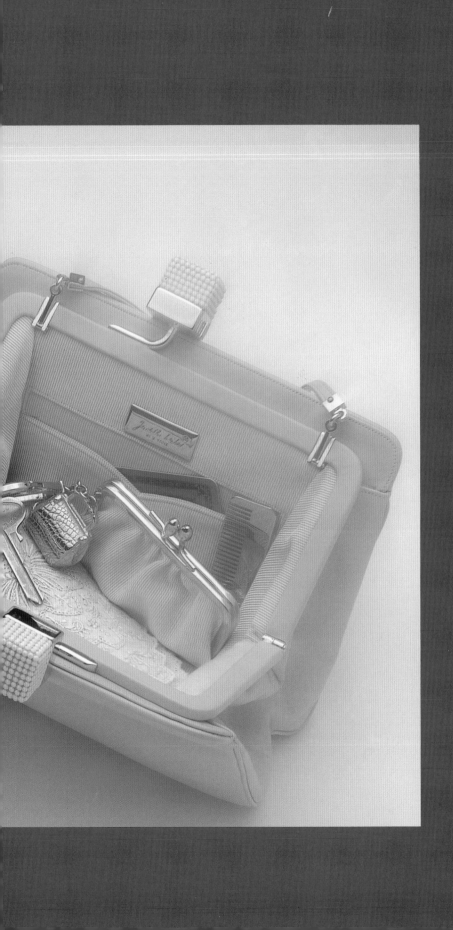

EVENING BAGS

Black alligator evening bag with rigid jet beaded handle, 1973.
From the collection of Margay Lindsey

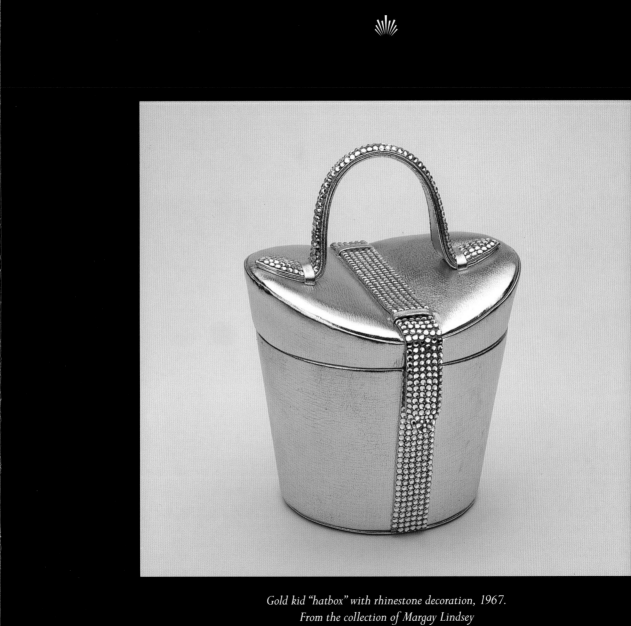

Gold kid "hatbox" with rhinestone decoration, 1967.
From the collection of Margay Lindsey

Jet bow lock on black alligator frame clutch, 1993

*Hummingbird lock on purple alligator clutch
with faux pearl closing, 1993*

*Multibow closing of jet and rhinestones on
black suede frame bag, 1991*

*Semiprecious and jet beaded lock on black suede
envelope, 1992*

*Dragonfly ornament with rhinestones on velvet envelope
with satin trim and passementerie handle, 1992*

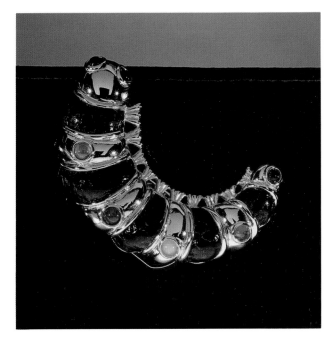

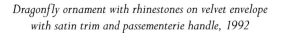

*Velvet frame clutch with dancing elephants decorated with rhinestones
and varicolored semiprecious stones, 1992*

Black satin hand-sewn frame bag with peacock ornaments and rhinestones, 1974. From the collection of Betty Gershman

Navy suede frame bag with double frog locks, 1993

Black patent leather frame clutch with semiprecious stones on bar,
drop-in shoulder strap, 1989.
From the collection of Barbara Bush

*Black karung snake gathered evening bag
with rhinestones and rosequartz details, 1979*

*Black velvet gathered frame pouch, gold-plated frame
with green and black enamel, rhinestone trim,
and drop-in gold chain, 1983*

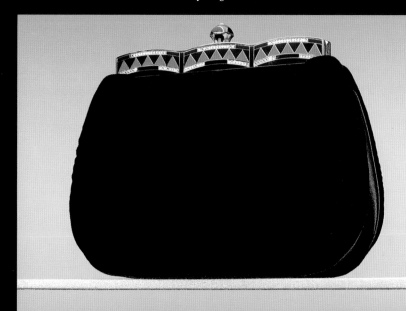

*Front and back of Japanese nineteenth-century obi re-embroidered on both sides
with colored and clear rhinestones, frame decorated with faux marcasites
and onyx stones, 1975*

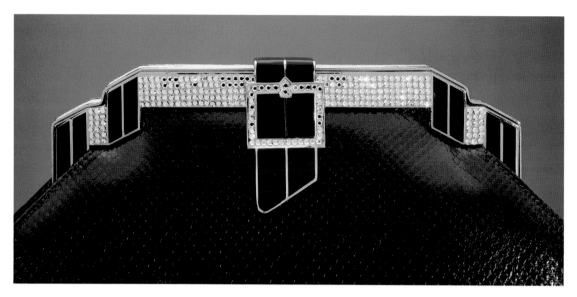

Enamel and rhinestone frame on black karung snake bag, 1991

Black, white, and red enamel frame on black alligator clutch, 1986

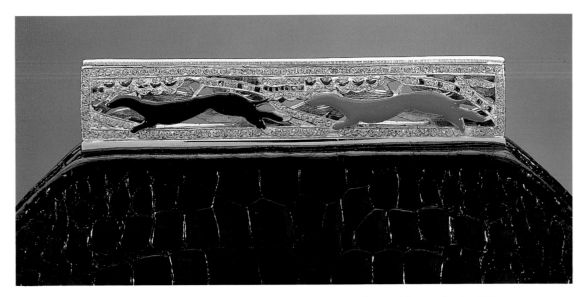

Faux marcasite red and black enamel greyhounds on lock of black alligator clutch, 1987

Black, red, and yellow enamel frame on black alligator clutch, 1986

Black satin clutch with Art Deco-inspired bar
with jet and rhinestones, 1973

Black satin evening bag with intricate rhinestone
and onyx decoration, 1979

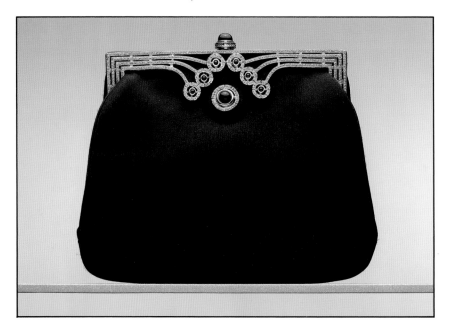

*Black satin elongated clutch on rhinestone onyx and chrysoprase
stone decorated frame, drop-in chain, 1981*

*Black satin frame clutch gathered on a rhinestone encrusted frame
with onyx and rosequartz stones, drop-in chain, 1992*

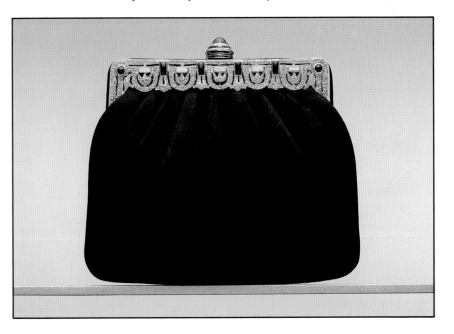

Multicolor paillette embroidered envelope with large tassel on side, 1993

Taffeta patchwork pouch, re-embroidered with multicolored rhinestones, 1991

*Front and back of shirred frame pouch, French
gold/green/fuchsia brocade re-embroidered
with multicolored rhinestones, 1992*

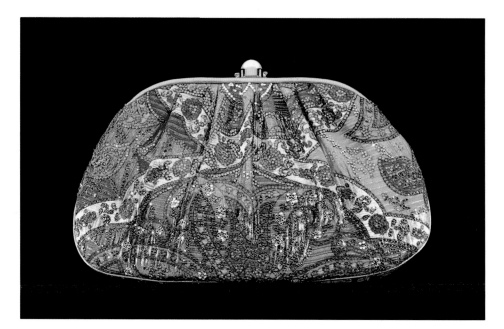

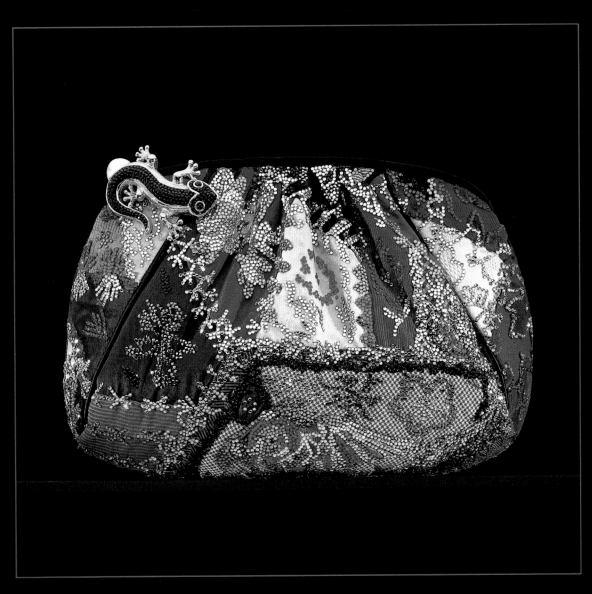

*Nineteenth-century American patchwork quilt re-embroidered
with multicolored rhinestones, 1993*

Rhinestone and patent leather decorated gate frame clutch
with geometric quilting on satin, 1977.
From the collection of Bernice Norman

Black satin frame bag with paisley embroidery faux and marcasite frame,
drop-in chain, onyx lock, 1988

*Black velvet pouch with passementerie embroidery
and marcasite-inspired frame, rhinestone and black onyx trim,
passementerie handle, 1991*

Japanese obi pouch, re-embroidered with rhinestones, 1990

*American cotton patchwork quilt, re-embroidered with rhinestones
and chalk beads, 1992*

MINAUDIÈRES

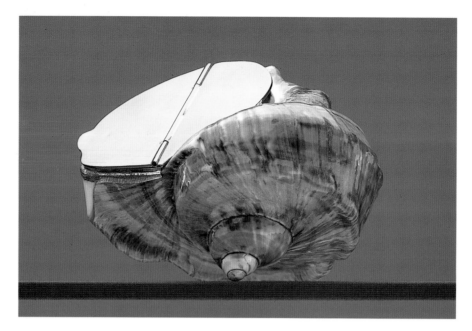

Natural green turbo shell with gold-plated lid
(Collection The Metropolitan Museum of Art, New York),
1972

Sea urchin with gold-plated lid
(Collection The Metropolitan Museum of Art, New York), 1972

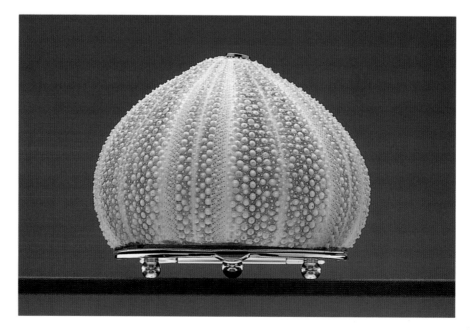

Shell bag with gold-plated frame, green onyx lock,
chain shoulder strap
(Collection The Metropolitan Museum of Art, New York), 1972

*Miser's bag-shaped minaudière, multicolored bouquet on rhinestone
ground, drop-in chain, 1992*

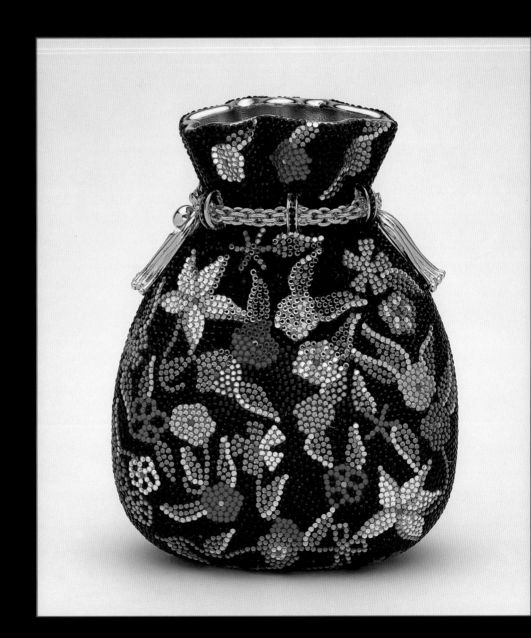

*Miser's bag-shaped minaudière, jet ground, multicolored flowers,
drop-in chain, 1991*

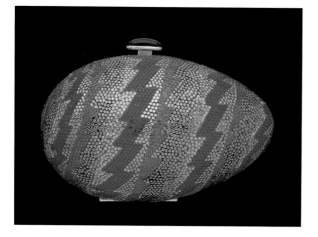

*Small multicolored "lightning" egg
with drop-in chain, 1971*

*Tiny egg with multicolored flowers on jet
ground, drop-in chain, 1993*

*Small lavender patterned egg with amethysts,
drop-in chain, 1970*

*Aztec patterned egg with onyx lock and
decorations, drop-in chain, 1991*

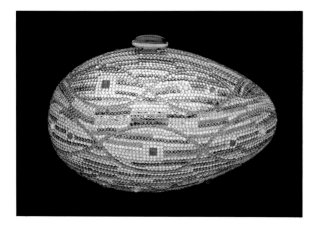

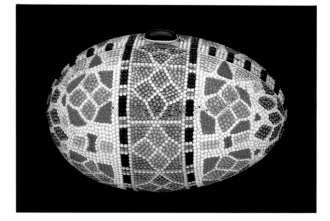

Black and white lightning-inspired egg with drop-in chain, 1994

Green/black gator-patterned egg, black onyx lock, drop-in chain, 1993

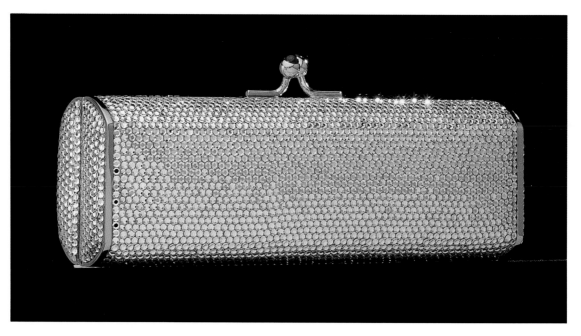

Hexagon-shaped oblong rhinestone-covered tiny box, garnets in lock, 1994

Rhinestone-encrusted box, inspired by Japanese rice bale, 1988

*Rhinestone leaves with ridged "yellow diamond" covered sections,
tassel handle, drop-in chain, 1992*

*Florentined gold-plated minaudière shaped like
a gift-wrapped box, 1993*

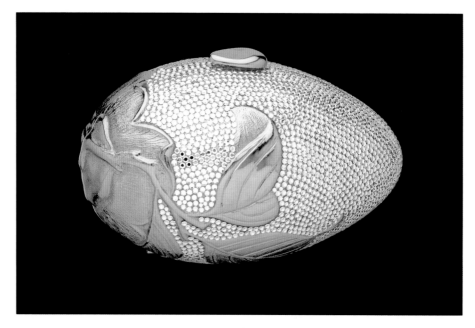

Small rhinestone egg with leaf design, drop-in chain, 1971

Egg-shaped box inspired by moon and stars, drop-in chain, 1990

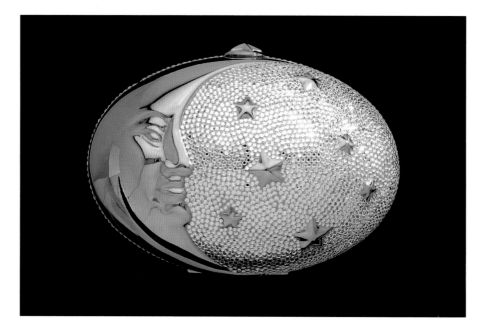

Gold wave design oval box, rhinestone-decorated band,
garnet lock, drop-in chain, 1992

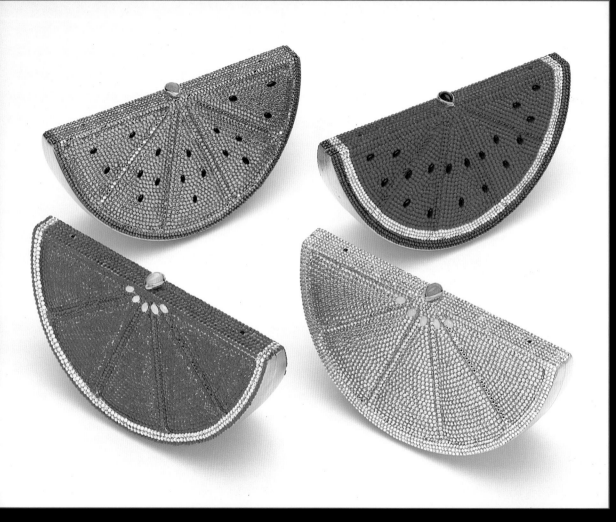

Watermelon, orange, lemon, and kiwi-shaped boxes, drop-in chain, 1991

Rose shaped minaudière encrusted with red, clear, and jonquil rhinestones,
drop-in chain, 1994

Eggplant box in purple, yellow, and orange rhinestones,
drop-in chain, 1988

"Chinese pillow" inspired by a baby with patchwork vest, 1988

Chinese foo dog in multicolored rhinestones, drop-in chain, 1985

Buddha shaped box with multicolored flower design
on rhinestone ground, drop-in chain, 1987

Beckoning cat, onyx lock, drop-in chain, 1994

Sleeping cat, jet polka dots, jet bow, 1984

Group of dog minaudières with pillbox, 1988

Fantasy zebra horse encrusted in jet, orange, and yellow rhinestones, 1979

Part beaded and florentined hand-engraved horse, 1979

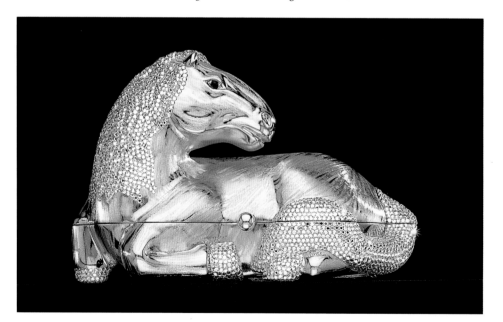

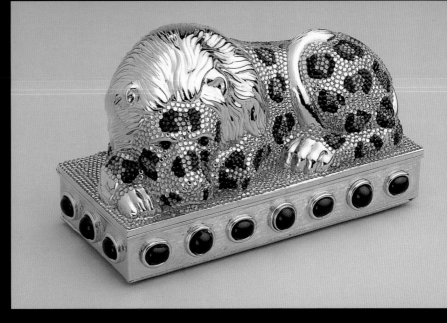

Resting lion box with leopard pattern, onyx stone border, 1978

Three ram's head boxes, all with drop-in chain, all 1991. Top: Chinese pattern; left and right: abstract pattern in jet / rhine and red / rhine

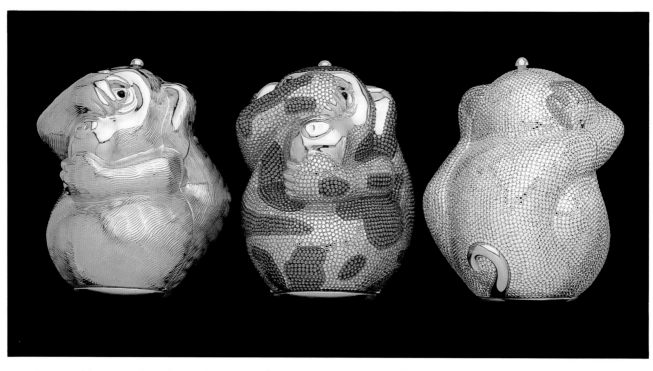

See no evil, hear no evil, speak no evil monkeys. Left: gold-plated; center: bronze, fur inspired; right: rhinestone covered. All 1992

Tutankhamen monkey, drop-in chain, 1989.
From the collection of Michelle Friman

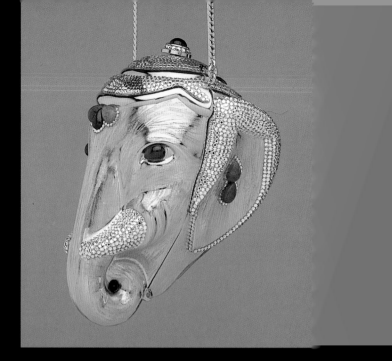

*Elephant box with rhinestone and semiprecious
stone trim (garnets, green onyx), 1988*

Rhinestone decorated stylized turtle box, with oval garnet in lock, drop-in c

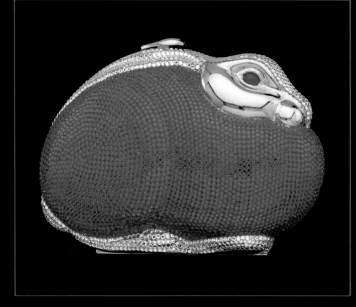

Red and rhinestone decorated rabbit, drop-in chain, 1969

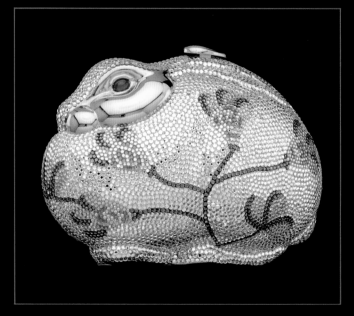

Floral patterned rabbit, drop-in chain, 1969

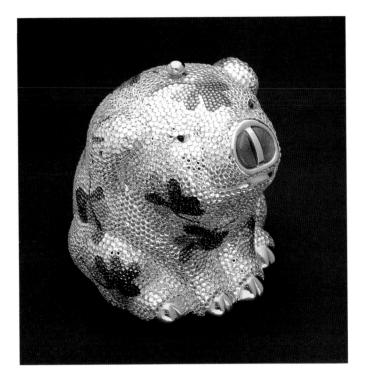

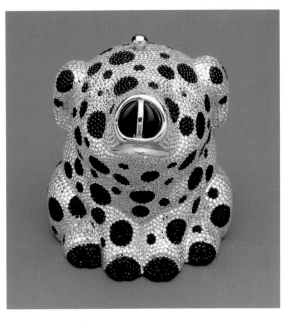

Rhinestone and green clover pig,
green onyx nose, drop-in chain, 1991

Jet polka-dot pig on rhinestone ground
with drop-in chain, 1991

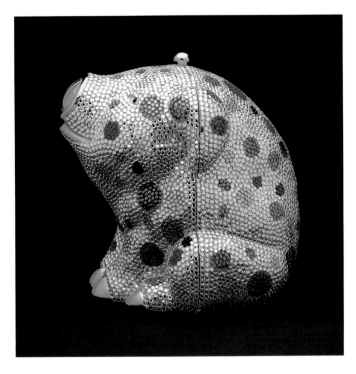

Multicolored polka-dot pig on rhinestone
ground with drop-in chain, 1991

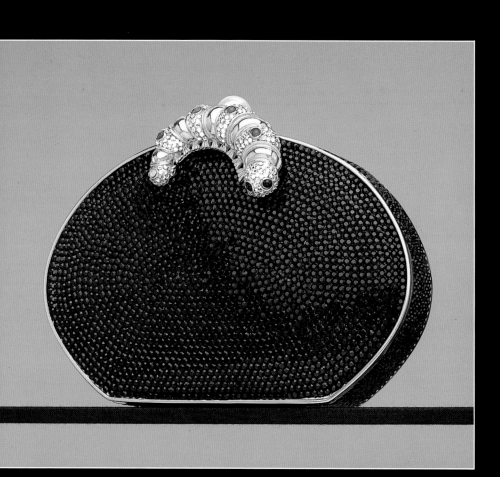

Jet bead minaudière with caterpillar lock, 1987

Left: jet oblong box with scattered semiprecious stones framed in rhinestones, drop-in chain, 1987;
Right: teardrop-shaped box jet encrusted, rhinestone snowflakes, onyx lock, drop-in chain, 1994

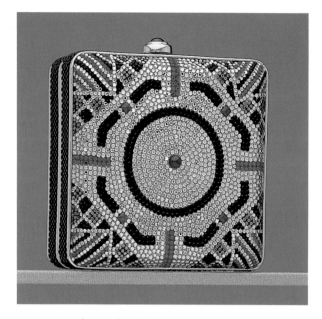

Square box, multicolored "watch"-inspired design in black, red, green, and "yellow diamond" color rhinestone ground, with onyx lock and drop-in chain, 1994

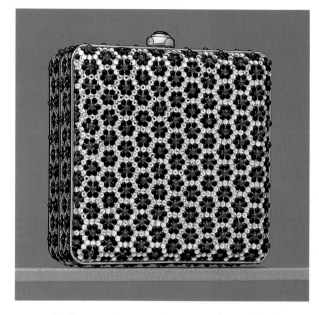

Small square box, jet and garnet with tiny floral pattern, onyx lock, and drop-in chain, 1990

Small square box, jet background, rhinestone trellis with garnets, garnet lock, drop-in chain, 1990

Small square box "Bridget Reilly"-inspired, jet and rhine beads, 1992

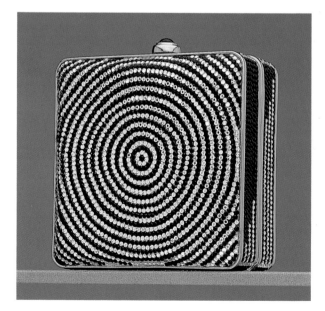

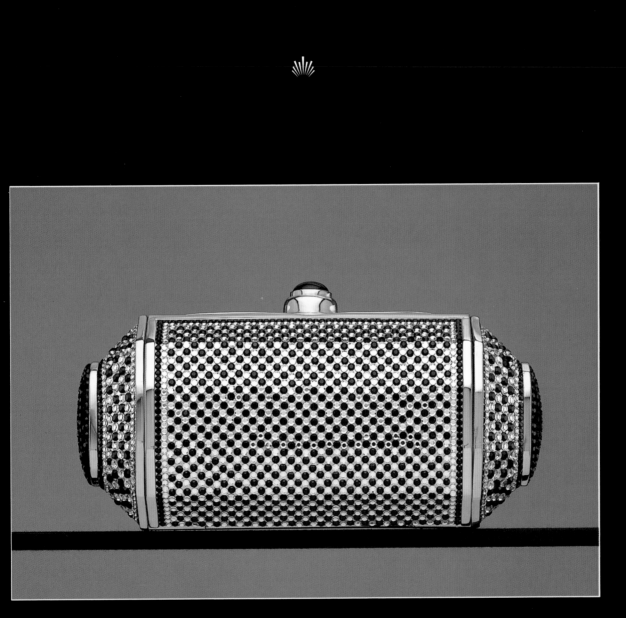

Jet / rhine dot beaded geometric box, drop-in chain, 1976

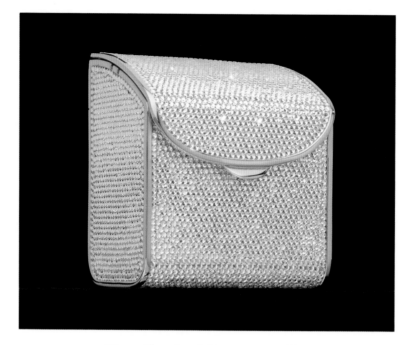

*Tiny mailbox-shaped rhinestone minaudière
with gold trim, drop-in chain, 1973*

*"Mask" box with drop-in chain, 1993.
From the collection of Alice Netter*

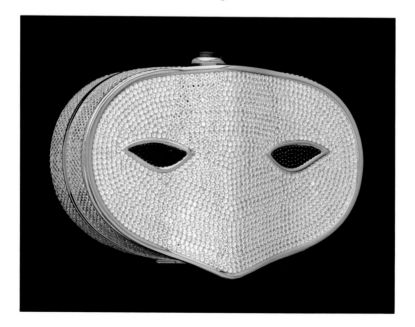

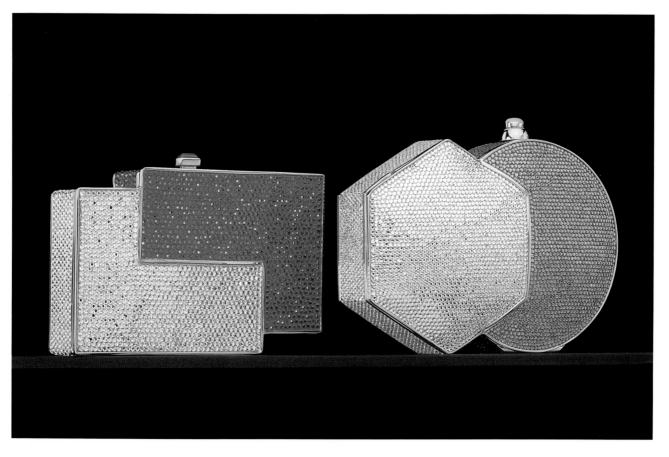

Geometric boxes in red / rhinestone; turquoise / rhinestone, 1985

Three patterned ball-shaped minaudières with tassels and passementerie cord handles, 1991

*Round box, "red lightning" aurum and jet stones, garnets in center,
drop-in chain, 1991*

*Multicolored tiny octagon-shaped box, onyx pyramid lock,
drop-in chain, 1993*

Pillow-shaped box, multicolored with onyx stones interspersed,
onyx lock, drop-in chain, 1994

Navajo-inspired rounded minaudière with onyx clasp,
drop-in chain, 1969

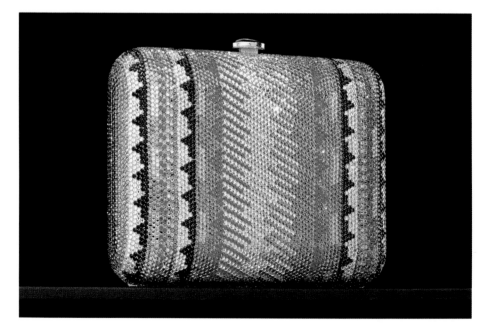

Computer graphics design rounded box, drop-in chain, 1988

*Patchwork quilt on "suitcase" style box,
drop-in chain, 1992*

Multicolored jazzy bow box, drop-in chain, 1993

Summer patchwork quilt-inspired rounded box,
garnet lock, drop-in chain, 1992

Jet ground flower garden, onyx lock, drop-in chain, 1992

Oblong minaudière inspired by an Oriental carpet, 1973

Oblong "Tiffany" box, 1973

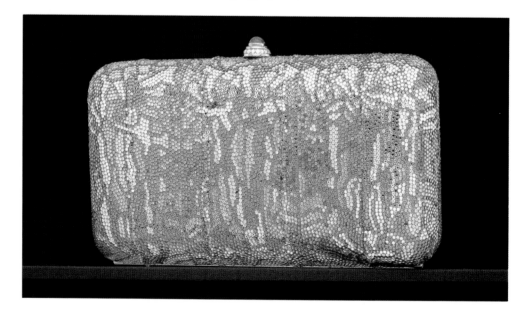

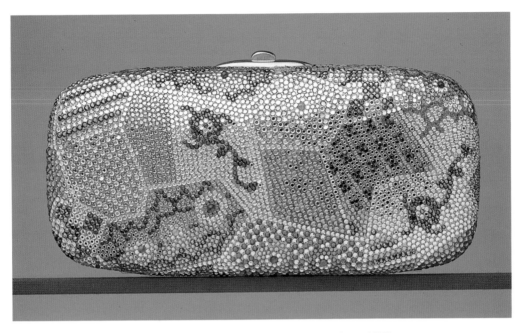

Oval box inspired by imari design, drop-in chain, 1973

"Multicolor" geometric design, drop-in chain, 1974

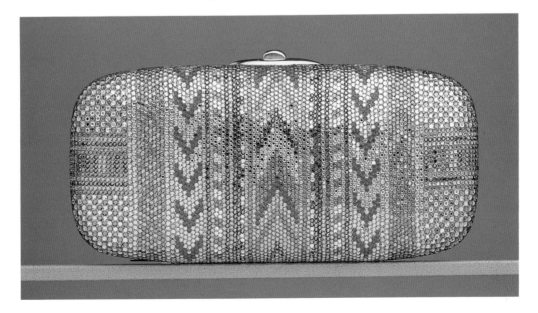

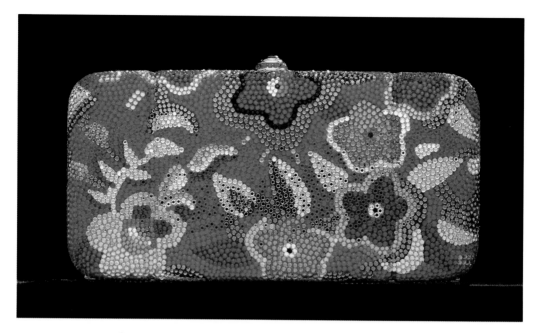

Romanian patterned oblong box, garnet lock, drop-in chain, 1992

Oblong minaudière, trellis and flowers, 1991

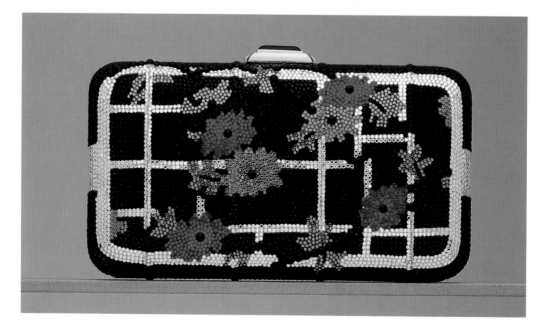

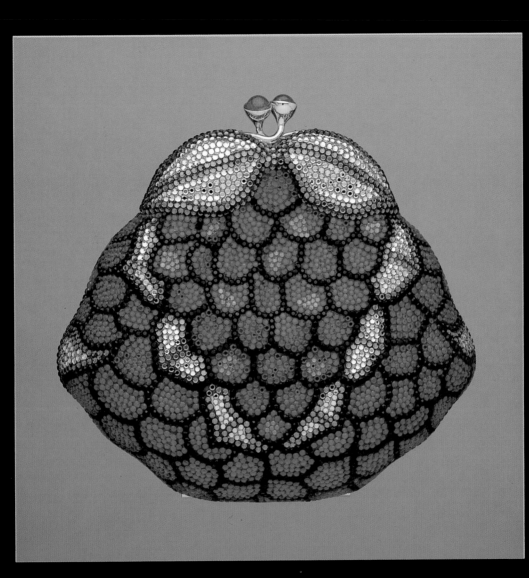

Bunch of grapes box, green onyx lock, drop-in chain, 1986

Leopard patterned stiff frame bag, 1991

Square frame evening purse, bronze and jet beaded sides in stylized leopard pattern, 1994

Rounded teardrop-shaped box with dragonfly pattern, onyx lock, drop-in chain, 1992